KENTISH TOWN
PAST

First published 1997
by Historical Publications Ltd
32 Ellington Street, London N7 8PL
(Tel: 0171-607 1628)

ISBN 0 948667 42 7
British Library Cataloguing-in-Publication Data
A catalogue record for this book is available from the British Library

Typeset in Palatino by Historical Publications Ltd
Reproduction by G & J Graphics, London EC2
Printed by Edelvives in Zaragoza, Spain.

Historical Publications specialises in local history books.
They would be happy to receive proposals for further titles in this series.

KENTISH TOWN
PAST

John Richardson

HISTORICAL PUBLICATIONS

Acknowledgements

I have had much help in writing this book from Malcolm Holmes, Borough Archivist of the London Borough of Camden, and from Richard Knight, Local Studies Manager and his colleagues, all at the Local History and Archives Centre at Holborn Library. As always, they have been efficient and co-operative.

I am also indebted to Gillian Tindall for information and the use of some previously unpublished prints; to Basil Leverton for his recollections and connections; to Paul Callan for information on Dr Stukeley and Gregory Bateman; to Ann Currie for new information on the Gordon House Academy; and to Simon Morris for his researches on the Junction Road. Other informants have included Roger Cline, Charles Nisbitt, Dr Pamela Taylor and Michael Ogden.

The Illustrations

I am grateful to the London Borough of Camden for permission to reproduce most of the illustrations in this book. Others were reproduced by courtesy of the following:

Peter Barber: *105*

Peter Jackson Collection: *42*

London Metropolitan Archives: *40, 41*

J. Sainsbury plc: *124*

St Pancras Housing Association: *107, 108, 109*

Gillian Tindall: *1, 7, 10, 13, 23, 43, 104*

The following were supplied by Historical Publications Ltd:
4, 5, 6, 9, 12, 15, 16, 17, 18, 20, 25, 26, 39, 45, 46, 47, 51, 53, 58, 59, 60, 61, 65, 69, 71, 74, 76, 78, 80, 88, 92, 93, 99, 101, 102, 106, 110, 117, 120, 135, 138, 140, 142, 153, 154, 156, 157, 158, 159, 160

1. 'A View from the Top of Kentish Town'. The location of this eighteenth-century view has not been identified.

The Early Village

TWO CENTRES

The single street that signified Kentish Town remained unextended until the closing years of the eighteenth century, when the first side streets were partially formed. A village outside the immediate lure of central London, Kentish Town was then of a familiar form: houses and hovels strung along the highway, a chapel, a number of elderly inns, a village green, and several private schools usually run by impecunious clergymen or by ladies without sufficient private income. The whole was surrounded by fields and, indeed, if the lack-lustre development of Camden Town had not begun in 1791, those fields would have extended uninterrupted all the way down to what is now Euston Road.

A traveller then might have assumed that Kentish Town, with its facilities and landmarks, was the seat and centre of a largely rural parish. In most ways it was, but there were pecularities about its status which were eventually to retard the development of local government in the area.

Kentish Town was, in fact, only part of the parish of St Pancras, though for centuries the two place names in official documents were synonymous and interchangeable. Sometimes these documents indicate that St Pancras was *in* Kentish Town and not the other way round. In 1788, when the lord of the manor of Cantelowes applied for permission to build on the empty acres of what became Camden Town, his Act was called the 'Kentish Town Act'.

It will thus be seen that the area *perceived* as Kentish Town was, before the nineteenth century, much larger than it is today and could stretch from St Pancras Old Church up to Parliament Hill Fields. It is a reflection of modern worries about property values that today Kentish Town residents would definitely not wish to have 'St Pancras' identified with their neighbourhood; nor conversely would many Gospel Oak house vendors own up to living in Kentish Town and would prefer, without historical justification, to snuggle up with Hampstead. These are vagaries of fashion and market values, but for the purpose of this book, up to the nineteenth century 'Kentish Town' will include the historical area down to St Pancras Old Church. After that Kentish Town is more closely confined to that area recognised today, from the railway bridge across the road near Camden Town up to Swains Lane. Any outraged residents in that latter area who might think of themselves as 'Highgate' are reminded that the mansion built in the eighteenth century on the site of St Alban's Villas was known as Kentish Town House, and Grove Terrace in Highgate Road was earlier known as 'Kentish Town Terrace'.

2. Kentish Town Farm House at today's junction of Caversham Road and Kentish Town Road. The building was probably built in the sixteenth century, perhaps on the site of an earlier building. It was demolished when the Christ Church Estate developed its land in the mid-nineteenth century. By then it was known as 'Morgan's Farm', from its last tenant, William Morgan.

The parish of St Pancras was narrow and elongated. It stretched from near today's Tottenham Court Road station in the south up to Highgate Village in the north. On the east it was bordered by the very old road from east of the present King's Cross station up to Highgate – once called Maiden or Midden Lane, and now York Way and Brecknock Road. On the west the boundary was less definite, meandering through Fitzrovia and Regent's Park up to Chalk Farm and over Parliament Hill to Kenwood.

The original parish church – now St Pancras Old Church in Pancras Road – is on a Roman site, one thought to have been used for their religious ceremonies. The church's location and its dedication to Pancratius, a Phrygian martyr popular in the earlier years of Christendom, suggest that it was a very early foundation indeed – perhaps as far back as the fourth century. In the usual course of things, the main village of the parish would have grown up around the church, but in St Pancras this does not appear to have happened. Certainly in medieval times there was a vicarage nearby and a number of dwellings. Not too far away was St Pancras Manor House, Cantelowes Manor House and possibly another mansion of some importance, strung along St Pancras Way, but the majority of the population lived in Kentish Town village a mile and a half distant. This is emphasised by the building of a chapel-of-ease somewhere in Kentish Town *c.*1200, and the rebuilding of that chapel in the middle of the fifteenth century on the west side of Kentish Town Road. It is likely that the vicar of St Pancras himself decamped to a new house in Kentish Town sometime after 1250[1].

The move away from the old church was both significant and practical. It confirmed and substantiated Kentish Town's supremacy in the parish, but most likely it was the practical advantages of the move which were decisive in obtaining permission to build a chapel-of-ease. The land and roadway near the old church were often flooded when the Fleet river, which flowed beside Pancras Road, overran its banks. A heavy rainstorm would send water rushing down from the heights of Highgate, overwhelming the confines of the stream at the aptly named Pancras Wash – the area near the church. In 1331 it was noted that the church was "undermined and destroyed by overflowings of the River Fleete", and as late as the

3. The view in Kentish Town Road, by Anglers Lane. Drawing by Samuel Hieronymous Grimm in the 1770s.

nineteenth century storms often flooded the homes of people at King's Cross when the culvert containing the river burst from the pressure. To compound the problem, the Fleet from long use and misuse had become silted up in its lower reaches, retarding its upstream flow.

Therefore, at a time when regular attendance at the parish church was important, the difficulties encountered on a trip to St Pancras, a church standing on a knoll above a swampy road, were a serious matter. How much worse then for the parishioners who lived in Highgate who, until the establishment of a hermit's chapel in their own village, had an even more unpleasant journey in difficult weather.

Inevitably, once St Pancras church lost much of its function the area around it declined and in 1593, in his *Speculum Britanniæ*, John Norden was able to say, in a frequently quoted passage:

"Pancras Church.... standeth all alone as utterly forsaken, old and wether-beaten, which for the antiquitie therof, it is thought not to yeeld to Paules in London: about this church have been manie buildings, now decaied, leaving poore Pancras without companie or comfort: yet it is now and then visited with Kentish towne and Highgate, which are

members thereof, but they seldom come there, for they have Chapels of ease within themselves, but when there is a corps to be interred, they are forced to leave the same in this forsaken church or churchyard, where (no doubt) it resteth as secure against the day of resurrection as if it laie in stately Paules." Norden later warns that the church area is visited by thieves "who assemble not there to pray, but to wait for praye, and manie fall into their hands, clothed, that are glad when they escape naked. Walk there not too late."

When that settlement around the old church was depleted and how large it was in its prime in comparison to the village of Kentish Town, is now difficult to assess. But it *is* possible to suggest that Kentish Town was *always* the hub of the parish, and always its principal village. Several factors point to this: firstly, as we have seen, the chapel-of-ease in Kentish Town was built as early as the thirteenth century, and the vicar moved there promptly. In a parish in which the population was minute this implies that the majority of residents were already in Kentish Town. Significant too is the location of the village green – an ancient creation essential to most parishes – it was *north* of Kentish Town beside Highgate Road.

4. *South view of St Pancras Old Church in 1815 before its 'modernisation'. The burial ground is much tidier than it probably was at the time. Pancras Road runs to the left and the Adam and Eve pub, with its tea gardens, is seen to the north.*

5. *Extract from a plan of Tottenhall Manor, made for Charles Fitzroy (later Lord Southampton) in 1761. The road running left to right is today's Highgate West Hill and Highgate Road. The village green is shown near the centre – today it is marked by the gardens opposite Grove Terrace.*

No record has emerged which indicates the existence of a communal green near the old church.

The abandonment of the old parish church and nearby buildings was not, in an archaeological sense, the desertion of a medieval village, for the main village of the parish already existed at Kentish Town. What probably happened at St Pancras was a gradual decline in the number of people who wished to live there.

The peculiarity of the parish church being at some distance from the main settlement at Kentish Town was most likely due to its very early foundation on a site already associated with religion: this was before topographical factors, such as soil quality and water supply, essential to the growth and comfort of the community, were of much consequence. If, as with most Middlesex parishes, the church had been founded in late Saxon times, it would have been placed in Kentish Town and probably dedicated to St Mary.

A CONFLICT OF INTERESTS

The problem for Kentish Town was that the ecclesiastical authorities did not acknowledge these topographical or demographic realities. They did not, so to speak, decommission the old church and transfer its status to Kentish Town Chapel. This neglect or

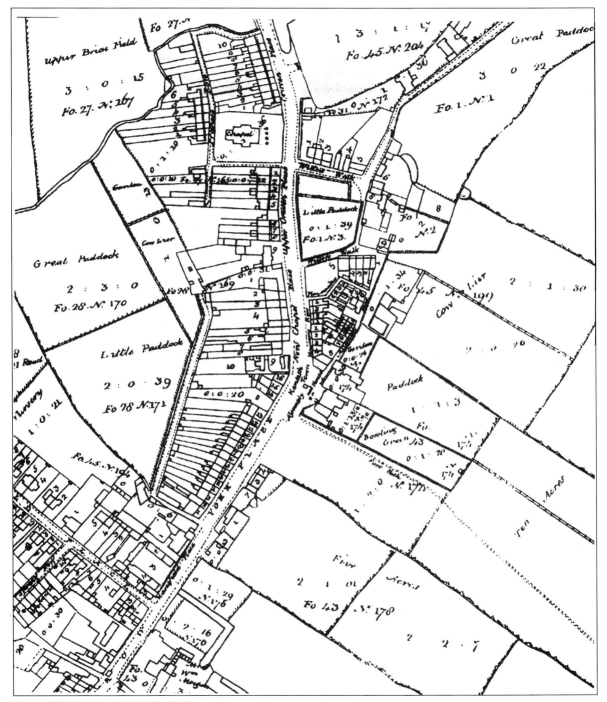

6. *Thompson's map of the parish of St Pancras, compiled about 1800. This section shows the main highway through Kentish Town – today's Kentish Town Road, leading up to the Assembly House and then along Highgate Road. In the centre of the picture there is a branch off the main road called Forteys Lane, which corresponds, at least at its southern end, with today's Fortess Road. Kentish Town Chapel, built in 1784, is to the top of the map.*

refusal thereby ensured that the customary fusion of local authority, influence and facilities in the parish, around the personages of the vicar and leading citizens, was always fractured. When, in the last half of the eighteenth century, population increased substantially in the southern part of the parish below the Euston Road, the residents of Kentish Town were faced with resentment from that quarter. For the people in the south had no adequate place of worship, and St Pancras Old Church was not only far too small for them to crowd into but in bad repair. Envious eyes were cast upon the convenience to Kentish Town residents of having their own chapel. This divisiveness was exacerbated when in 1784 Kentish Town Chapel was replaced by a new church further up the road, which building forms the kernel of the present St John the Baptist[2] in Highgate Road. The cost of building this went over budget and in 1785 a move to levy a supplementary rate of 7d in the £ to pay for the remaining expenses was heavily defeated by a now intransigent open St Pancras Vestry. Though this decision was overturned the following year, the matter went to court and it was not until 1793 that the action of the Church Lands Trustees in building the new church in Kentish Town was legally upheld. In that same year, the vicar was roundly condemned for neglecting the Old Church where for many years divine service had been held only once a month. As was pointed out to him, nine tenths of the rate income of the parish was then derived from the southern part of it[3] and the vicar's more frequent appearance in the old building was therefore justified and required.

The residents of the Tottenham Court Road area had right on their side – the parish church had been overlooked, and it was that building which most urgently needed rebuilding or enlarging.

These matters encouraged a divide between the north and south of the parish which was to bedevil Vestry politics and lead to disputes and municipal upheaval. As time went on, the assumption of Kentish Town to be the heart of the parish was undermined and in the nineteenth century erased altogether. The symbol of municipal power – the Vestry Offices – was built, not in Kentish Town in whose pubs and chapel the Vestry had once met, but next

7. 'At Kentish Town', by Samuel Hieronymous Grimm, published in 1780. The house has not yet been identified.

8. *This picture is alleged to be of Cain Place, Kentish Town. Cain Place formed the apex at the southern entrance to Kentish Town, fronting both Royal College Street and Kentish Town Road – it is in fact the subject of the illustration on the front of the jacket of this book. However, the buildings in the two pictures do not bear comparison.*

to St Pancras Old Church, despite the fact that the St Pancras area was by then squalid and disreputable. And in 1822 when the old parish church was at last replaced, it was located not in Kentish Town but on the south side of Euston Road. Kentish Town never did develop as the administrative heart of the parish and in time it became just a part, and not a particularly prosperous part, of one of the most overbuilt and over-populated parishes in London.

In the nineteenth century Kentish Town was filled out by a mass of third-rate housing which inevitably decreased its social status, but apart from the swathes of land taken up by railway companies, there was little industry or manufacture to go with it. Kentish Town could not therefore compete with the commercial and cultural importance of the south of the parish, nor even with the upstart Camden Town. In addition, the socially superior residents of Highgate, traditionally allies of Kentish Town, gradually withdrew from local politics, leaving Kentish Town even more isolated.

Manors and Estates

DIVIDED BY MANORS

In medieval times vestry meetings were no more than a gathering of leading residents in the vestry room of the church, chaired by the vicar, which discussed parish business, the church fabric and burial ground, administered charitable bequests and generally dealt with the poor and destitute. Away from this the real business of life was handled by the manors. The manor courts dealt with the ownership and transfer of land, management of agriculture, maintenance of roads and streams, and the disorderly behaviour of residents. Two manors divided Kentish Town – Cantelowes and Tottenhall, neatly separated by the line of today's Camden High Street and Kentish Town and Highgate Roads, with Cantelowes on the east. The records of Cantelowes have been largely edited and add greatly to our knowledge of the customs and development of that part of Kentish Town, but those of Tottenhall are only now being transcribed under the aegis of the Camden History Society.

The popular concept of a lord of the manor governing local society with the aid of vicar, churchwardens and other local worthies is, in the case of Kentish Town, inapplicable. Not only was the village divided between two manors, but the manorial lords were absentee, since, as with many villages around London, the manors were owned by prebendaries of St Paul's Cathedral. Business at manor courts was conducted on behalf of St Paul's by stewards who may or may not have been locally resident. With the landlords and possibly their stewards absent, there was no constant presence of civil authority in the form of a local 'squire' and civic leadership was spread amongst the larger landowners who wished to be bothered. As with Kentish Town's ecclesiastical status, the situation was flawed.

The court rolls of Cantelowes exist from 1480 until modern times, with an exasperating gap of 54 years in the sixteenth century and some omissions in the next century. There were two kinds of court – the baron and the leet. The former dealt with the transfer and management of land, the latter with the appointment of unpaid officials and the minor misdemeanours of tenants. The neglect of such things as blocked-up streams, highway repairs and dunghills on the waste were the concern of the court baron.

Not much of Cantelowes was held freehold. A large chunk, what eventually became Camden Town (east of the High Street) and its extension to York Way, was the lord's demesne land – territory which in theory he farmed himself and on which the other tenants of the manor had to work at various times

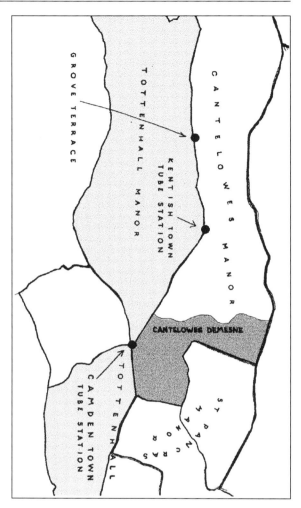

9. *A simplified plan of the manors of north St Pancras, showing Cantelowes on the east of what became Camden High Street and Kentish Town Road, and Tottenhall to the west of it. Other manors in the parish included Rugmere to the far left, most of which was taken by Henry VIII for his hunting park (now Regent's Park) and the rest seems to have become part of Tottenhall. The lay and prebendal manors of St Pancras, by the Old Church, have left few records.*

Cantelowes came into the possession of Charles Pratt in the eighteenth century. When ennobled, he chose the name Lord Camden after his house at Chislehurst, and when he developed his estate in Cantelowes it became known as Camden Town.

10. *'Old House adjoining the manor house Kentish Town belonging to the University of Cambridge'. This undated drawing depicts a house on the estate belonging to St John's College Cambridge, land between Leighton Road on the south and the railway to the north. The significance of 'adjoining the manor house' is discussed on page 22.*

of the year. Any tenant of these fields or of any premises on them therefore dealt directly with the lord's steward and do not appear in the court rolls. Illustration 9 shows the extent of the manor and the approximate area of the demesne land.

Almost all of the land north of Camden Town up to Highgate was copyhold, a term which arose from the lord of the manor having one copy of the tenancy agreement and the tenant another. The letting and inheritance of copyhold land forms the main business of the court baron records and it is possible to trace the ownership and long development of many pockets of property in Kentish Town. This applies, for example, to the land in Highgate Road which contains St Alban's Villas and La Sainte Union Convent–ownership records go back to 1480. Though tenants were able to sell, mortgage and bequeath their tenancies, just as with a freehold, they were able to do so only with the permission of the lord, who would demand a fee for his acquiesence. Unusually, in Cantelowes inheritance was by a custom called gavelkind, common in Kent and a few areas of London such as Haringey. By this property did not, as was usual, descend to the eldest son (or daughter in the absence of sons) if the tenant died intestate, but

equally to all children with a share to their mother. In this way landholdings were often fragmented, though sometimes arrangements were made for siblings to consolidate the inherited parts.

Three large estates in Kentish Town were bequeathed to institutions – St Bartholomew's Hospital and St John's College, Cambridge in the seventeenth century and another, just south of Kentish Town station, went to Christ Church, Oxford in the eighteenth century. These benefactions account for many Kentish Town street names. Small fields were the basis of charitable bequests, such as the area of Fortess Road; and others supported the upkeep of St Pancras Old Church. All these estates were of great importance in the development of Kentish Town.

It is apparent from Cantelowes court records that the manor dealt with minor infringements of acceptable behaviour. In 1490 and 1496 men were fined for fighting and drawing blood, and in the sixteenth century men were arraigned for keeping 'loose women of evil conversation and conduct', for 'committing adultery, to the evil example of the King's lieges', and in the seventeenth century for permitting gaming (ninepins) in an alehouse yard, and for entertaining cripples and vagabonds in a barn. In 1691 appears the only reference to the lord extracting a 'deodand' from a tenant. This term referred to a law that if an unnatural death was caused by anything other than another person, that cause – even if inanimate – could be taken by the lord. In that year a horse which had thrown a child and then killed it with its hoof was impounded by the lord.

By the eighteenth century the influence of the manor courts was on the wane as government gave more powers to the vestries. In 1725 St Pancras Vestry reported that Cantelowes had given away or sold waste and common land 'to the great prejudice of the inhabitants and the poor'. It was here referring particularly to land fronting the east side of Highgate Road, where what had previously been odd plots of waste ground on which landless people grazed animals, had been granted to tenants who then enclosed them for building purposes. The Vestry empowered churchwardens, overseers, constables and any other inhabitant to tear down such enclosures without risk of prosecution. It is not reported what then happened, but certainly enclosures on that particular stretch of wasteland continued.

Tenants were much less obsequious as that century went on. In 1740 the lord's court fined the lord himself (Nicholas Jeffreys) the high sum of £5 for not allowing sufficient wine to the court jury, and the following year another £5 for not repairing two bridges.

THE GREEN AND COMMON

Vestiges still remain of Kentish Town's green and common land – they face each other at Grove Terrace in Highgate Road. The pathway in front of Grove Terrace is, as local residents know, a continuation of an alleyway called College Lane that runs parallel to Highgate Road down to just north of Burghley Road – all the land between that alley and the main road was common or waste land.

Highgate Road was once called Green Street – a name that survives in the quaint Little Green Street, which runs off it today. The Green was probably only on the west side of the road, extending back to the field which now contains the Lido. Until the Tottenhall court rolls are transcribed it is not possible to know this for certain or when the large and handsome houses that formed 'The Grove', opposite Grove Terrace, were constructed. Only one of those houses survives today; most were lost, including Clevedon House, to the erection of mansion flats *c.*1900, and another sacrificed for a particularly crass borough council development on the corner of Gordon House Road.

11. *Looking north from Kentish Town Road, with the inn sign of the Castle pub on the left (the actual building is set back from the road). Drawing by Samuel Hieronymous Grimm, 1772.*

12. *Little Green Street in the 1930s. This tiny street, leading to the even narrower College Lane, is a reminder of the time when Highgate Road, called Green Street, led to the village green opposite Grove Terrace.*

THE VESTRY IN KENTISH TOWN

The records of St Pancras Vestry survive from 1718. They show a confused transition from simple open meetings of ratepayers who cared to turn up, to the time when the Vestry became an elected borough council at the end of the nineteenth century. The early Vestry usually met in Kentish Town, either at the Chapel or at pubs, or else they convened at the former and more comfortably continued at the latter, usually at what are now the Assembly House, Black Horse and the Jolly Anglers. It is interesting to note that the first use of the name Assembly House (rather than its old name of Bull or Black Bull) in the licensing records is for 1784, the same year that the much disputed new Kentish Town Chapel opposite was opened. Here we have, perhaps, Kentish Town asserting itself in as the ecclesiastical *and* social centre of the parish.

Vestry meetings could not have taken long, judging by the minutes – the administration of a few charities, the election of officers (all unpaid) and the occasional management decision regarding the churchyard usually filled the agenda. The open vestry continued in this congenial form until the growing number of poor in the parish necessitated a change which was to cause rancour in the parish for a very long time to come. These matters are properly the subject of an overall St Pancras history, but a brief summary of how the Vestry dealt with the poor would be useful in connection with Kentish Town.

Before the establishment of workhouses the poor were supported from parish rates, but generally left in their own homes if they had them, or else billetted on families. Orphaned or abandoned children were fostered and then apprenticed if they were boys. But the death rate among young children was very high indeed, especially if they were nursed, as many were, by very poor local women. The burial registers of St Pancras are full of references in the early eighteenth century to these women, many of whom lived in Kentish Town, and their unfortunate charges. The administration of all this was in the hands of two Overseers of the Poor, unpaid residents appointed by rote, whose hearts were probably not in the job and who would have been keen to save every penny they could of the ratepayers' money.

In 1731 the Vestry opened what its minutes imply was its first workhouse[1] in a house in St Pancras Way[2], and in 1772 this was superseded by a more commodious house on the site of today's Camden Town underground station. By 1802 the numbers of poor in need far exceeded the ability of the administration to collect the necessary funds. It was found that from the greatly enlarged population the Vestry had failed to collect each year the substantial sum of over £2,000 in poor rates. After petitioning Parliament a number of prominent ratepayers were able to establish a body called the Directors of the Poor which raised a rate of its own choosing via a reluctant open vestry, and employed collectors to administer the system. The Directors and the Vestry were at loggerheads thereafter, especially once a third workhouse was erected in 1809 near to St Pancras churchyard.

In 1819 residents opposed to the Directors obtained permission to form a Select Vestry which not only did away with the old open vestry at which most ratepayers could attend, but was established as a self-perpetuating body. This was not unusual then – such vestries existed in other newly urban parishes, but Parliament in this instance allowed the Directors to remain in being, so that the Select Vestry still had little control over expenditure on the poor. By then a good deal of the parish was built upon, particularly south of the Euston Road, but north of that Somers Town was formed and Camden Town was expanding on both sides of the High Street. Because St Pancras Vestry lacked the powers (indeed, had not tried to obtain them) the residential side roads of the parish were not looked after and eventually 25 Paving Boards, formed by the developers of the various estates, had charge of these roads, often erecting bars and gates to stop through traffic. In Kentish Town for example, the Holmes Estate on the west side of Kentish Town Road was responsible for paving and road maintenance in that area. In this muddled way St Pancras lurched through much of the nineteenth century.

Elusive Houses

The whereabouts of three large and ancient 'Kentish Town' houses has puzzled local historians for some time.[1] These are the manor houses for both St Pancras manor and Cantelowes manor, and the mansion belonging to William Bruges, the first Garter King of Arms, who entertained royalty here in 1416. (Tottenhall's manor house was at the junction of Hampstead Road and Euston Road.)

The position of St Pancras Manor House is the easiest to resolve. A document of 1707[2] notes that the parish that year was obliged by the Crown to repair the highway leading from the 'north corner of the wall of Pancras Manor House to the Castle Inn [in Kentish Town], being half a mile in length'. The order referred to what is now St Pancras Way, then classified as a 'king's way' – until 1937 St Pancras Way was called King's Road. St Pancras manor and its manor house were on the east side of St Pancras Way between Agar Grove and St Pancras Old Church. Half a mile down from the Castle would place the house just south of Agar Grove, roughly where the

canal cuts under the road, and where in the late eighteenth century a mansion called Elm Lodge was built for the lessee of what was then left of the manor. The location of this house was as far away from the Old Church and as near to Kentish Town as was possible within the boundaries of the manor landholding – perhaps a further piece of evidence that Kentish Town was *the* village in the parish. The same document describes the house, then still standing, as 'a three gabled Mansion of wood and plaister': illustration 13, which has only recently been discovered, confirms this, and its caption tells us that it was occupied by Martin Folkes (1690-1754), President of the Royal Society from 1741 to 1753. The date of the illustration is 1751, but there is no sign of such a building on the detailed map of the parish of *c*.1800.

CANTELOWES MANOR HOUSE

The locating of Cantelowes manor house, however, is beset by choices. It seems at first straightforward. In a survey of the manor made in 1649[3] the 'manor house called Cantlers' is quite plainly within the lord

13. *'A Drawing of The Manor House of Pancrass residence of my father Martin Folkes Esqr. given to Ellen by me on the 9th of Nov 1751'. Folkes was President of the Royal Society from 1741 to 1753. St Pancras Manor House was on the east side of St Pancras Way, just south of Agar Grove.*

of the manor's own farm land – the demesne land. This would be both usual and logical. It has already been noted (p.14) that the demesne land was east of Camden High Street, extending beyond St Pancras Way to York Way. There seems little doubt, by comparing the details of the 1649 Survey and the fields shown on the *c*.1800 map[4], that the manor house was on the west side of St Pancras Way, almost opposite St Pancras Manor House. A small farm building is shown on the 1800 map opposite today's Agar Grove, but I suspect that the manor house was slightly down from this, south of today's Baynes Street.

My principal reason for this conjecture is based on an eighteenth-century sketch of the 'Workhouse Kentish Town' (Illustration 14), to be found in the Heal Collection at Holborn Library. This depicts a man fishing in the Fleet river, with St Pancras church in the distance and, presumably, a road to the left of the picture running in front of the house. This conjunction of river, road and view of the church, shown in map form in Illustration 15, occurs only in what in 1800 was the Bowling Green Field, on the west side of St Pancras Way. This is the very same field (though unnamed) which in the 1649 Survey mentioned above contained the Cantelowes manor house. John Rocque's unreliable map of 1746 places the workhouse at around this point, but it is difficult to be sure which side of the road he is indicating.

But if that is where the first workhouse was, where then was the former Cantelowes Manor House? My conclusion is that the first workhouse and the manor house were one and the same building. According to the Vestry minutes of 1736, when the Vestry renewed its lease of the building in which they housed the poor, it was rented from a 'Mr Jeffreys', then the lord of the manor. In my view, it is most unlikely that two substantial buildings would be crowded into the same field and the name, Bowling Green Field, implies the leisured life of a previously well-appointed house nearby. If my deduction is correct then we have in this drawing of the workhouse the only known depiction of Cantelowes Manor House which, judging from its exposed cross and vertical framework beams, was a very old building. Any remains are just south of the canal which skirts the car park of Reachview Court off Baynes Street.

It should be said that the church building in the distance looks not only like St Pancras Old Church, but also uncannily like Kentish Town Chapel as well, as comparison with Illustration 24 shows! But for various reasons, detailed in footnote 6, it seems unlikely that it could be the Chapel.

14. An undated sketch of the 'Workhouse Kentish Town'. The location is discussed in the text above.

vvorkhouse kentish Town

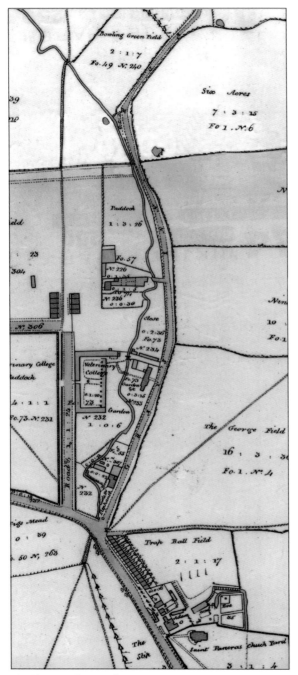

15. *Thompson's map of c.1800. Bowling Green Field is at the top and St Pancras Old Church at the bottom – the reverse of the viewpoint in Illustration 14. The river Fleet meets the road at the bottom of Bowling Green Field. It is suggested that the angler is in the Field on the east bank of the Fleet, with the house to the south of him.*

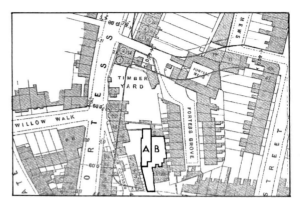

16. *Extract from a plan prepared by St Pancras Department of Works in 1889 showing the proposed widening of Fortess Road. For the sake of clarity, the words 'Cantelowes Manor House' and 'Manor Cottages', have been replaced by A and B in this reproduction.*

OTHER CONTENDERS

Yet there have been other claims for the location of Cantelowes manor house. In two mid-nineteenth century sketches, which have been discovered only in the last two years (illustrations 10 and 104), the captions beneath quite specifically say that the buildings depicted are near the old manor house at Kentish Town. One picture is of the temporary Roman Catholic church off the east side of Highgate Road, and the 'University of Cambridge' building in the other caption refers to a house on the St John's College Estate which stretches from the back of Leighton Road up to the railway crossing Highgate Road. Clearly then, a manor house, or a reputed manor house, was near Fortess Road. This is confirmed by an official plan drawn up in 1889 (ill. 16) when Fortess Road was to be widened. It marks a long house east of Fortess Road (opposite today's Tally-ho) as 'Cantelowes Manor House', and some dwellings nearby are called Manor Cottages. A house is shown at this location on the 1800 map.

It could be construed from this that Cantelowes manor decided at some time that the old manor house in St Pancras Way was too problematical as a building, or too far away from the village to serve as a manor house and another residence near the centre of the village was utilised instead. This suggestion is supported by a Parliamentary Survey of St Pancras properties, copied by Ambrose Heal and left in his remarkable collection of St Pancras material now at Holborn Library.[6] Unfortunately, he did not say where the original document was and I have been unable to trace it. The wording is rather ambiguous, but there is a reference to an 'appurtenance lying in Kentish Town next to the Manor House being now a garden plot containing there also those 11 acres of land called Base Court next Haymans and the three marshes now or late in the occupation of William Platt or his assignees'. Haymans was a landholding near Fortess Road (a row of cottages called Haymans Row was built just north of the Assembly House in the eighteenth century), and William Platt was the man who left his estate to St John's College, Cambridge. This seems conclusively to point to a manor house in the Fortess Road area. The trouble is that Mr Heal's copy of the Parliamentary Survey is dated 1650, only a year after another Parliamentary Survey (discussed above) makes it fairly clear that the manor house was on the demesne land in St Pancras Way.

If this were not confusing enough, another Cantelowes Manor House has often been suggested. This was a large farmhouse located exactly where Caversham Road joins Kentish Town Road. It was a Tudor building, as may be seen from many prints (see, for example, ill. 2) and towards its end was known as Morgan's Farm, when it was held for many years by an irascible farmer called William Morgan. However, its history may be traced back to at least

17. St George and William Bruges.

1594, when this 'capital messuage' was sold to a member of the Hewitt family. It was later part of the lands left by a Dr South to Christ Church, Oxford. There are a number of reasons, too complex to describe here, why this house could not have been the Cantelowes manor house, but suffice it to say that the house was in 1594 a copyhold tenancy, and could not have been the lord of the manor's own house, which would have been freehold.

A JUNKET IN KENTISH TOWN

An enormous feast was consumed at a house in Kentish Town in 1416 when William Bruges (1375?-1450), the first Garter King of Arms, entertained at his own house the Emperor Sigismund during his state visit to England. Bruges was responsible, as his successor is today, for the registration and supervision of grants of heraldic arms, and at that time had considerable social clout. He had attended the installation of the Emperor the previous year and this feast was probably by way of return hospitality.

The occasion was both magnificent and lavish, for the guests included not only the Emperor, but representatives from London's livery companies together with the Lord Mayor and aldermen, the king's trumpeters, officers-at-arms, esquires and knights, the Bishop of Ely, the Prince of Hungary and the Dukes of Briga and Holland, together with their retainers. Bruges knelt bareheaded to receive this cavalcade and escorted them to his house where minstrels and sackbutts diverted them. The food included nine pigs, seven sheep, one hundred pullets, one hundred pigeons, thirty capons and twenty hens, hares, rabbits, kids, salmon, eels, crabs, oysters, wild boars and red deer. If they stayed the night, unable to move from the excess of all this, then no doubt the distinguished personages had beds in the house and the rest camped in the fields around.

Where was Bruges' house? Was it in Kentish Town village or was the reference to Kentish Town in a medieval document an alternative to St Pancras?

Despite the uncertainty of its location, we know quite a bit about the house, for it crops up in two documents of the eighteenth century. The first is a journal of sorts kept by a local magistrate, William Woodhouse, who lived *c.*1704-08 in what he knew to be Bruges' old house, in the manor of Cantelowes. By then the building was half habitable but sufficient remained for Woodhouse to identify the private chapel that Bruges mentioned in his will and various coats of arms including those of Bruges and his son-in-law, who followed him as Garter King. Woodhouse boasted of a freehold life interest in the house, together with 45 acres of land, cottages and barns, though he does not say if the land etc. was freehold, copyhold or merely rented. In the same book he gives

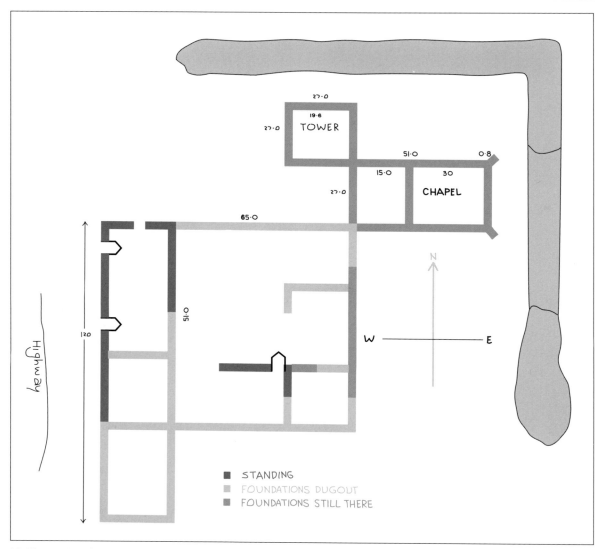

18. The remains of a house in St Pancras Way. This is redrawn from a copy of the plan in the Heal Collection, originally made by an unknown person in 1727.

details of the approximately sixteen houses on his Kentish Town estate which he himself let out.

The other document was penned by an unknown person in 1727[7]. The author of this had been interested enough to view and measure the remains of an old stone house east of a highway in the St Pancras/Kentish Town area. It contains a ground plan and a descriptive text. Measurements given here and in the Woodhouse account leave no doubt that this plan refers to the house that Woodhouse lived in, only about 19 years previously, and therefore to Bruges' residence. The plan is reproduced in Illustration 18,

and it shows the house east of the 'London to Haringay parc' road, with the hall fronting the highway; to the north is a square tower, with walls four feet thick, and a rectangular chapel adjacent.

To the north and east are the remains of a moat. In 1446 Bruges was granted permission by the king to take a 20ft strip off the road along the whole frontage in order to make a ditch at the front of the building. This implies that the road was a king's highway, needing the Crown's permission. He appears not to have done this work, for the next owner of the house was regranted the permission.

19. Extract from James King's Panorama of Kentish Town, showing the east side of St Pancras Way. In his commentary King describes the remains of the stone building as formerly a workhouse. The pronounced field boundary adjacent marks the beginning of the manor of St Pancras to the south.

We do not know if the highway side of the moat was ever constructed – it would, by that time, have been a decorative and traditional feature, rather than defensive.

Woodhouse states that his house was in Cantelowes, but nowhere in the court records for that period does he appear, nor do any of the names of his tenants that he notes in his journal. As he had 45 acres and about sixteen houses, their absence suggests that he and they were not on the copyhold lands, which extended from Highgate to today's Bartholomew Road. The non-copyhold lands on the east side of St Pancras Way extended from Bartholomew Road to just south of Agar Grove. On this hypothesis we may place the Bruges/Woodhouse house on that short section of St Pancras Way. Significantly, perhaps, that stretch is bordered by a large field called Hall Field on the c.1800 map, though no house is then shown. When James King drew his panorama of Kentish Town in the nineteenth century he showed the remains of a stone building at about this point (ill. 19), right up against the boundary line of Cantelowes manor[8]. He described his sketch as the ruins of 'Old St Pancras Work House', though as we have seen earlier the eighteenth-century sketch (ill.

14) of the workhouse indicates a wood beamed house, rather than a stone one, located on the west side of the road. But certainly the bit of house depicted by King, with its stone arch, appears to be an ancient structure. It could, indeed, be Bruges' house, the one later inhabited by Woodhouse.

For all that, there is some doubt, because though Woodhouse might be absent from the court rolls, Bruges is not. In 1487 Richard Ive (we know from other records that on his death in 1450 the Bruges house was sold to a Thomas Ive) surrendered a 19 acre croft called Deconnesfield, 'late of William Bruges', to his daughter Thomasine. This croft, to the east of Highgate Road, was eventually part of the St John's College estate. Other bits of land held by Bruges' heirs also feature in the court rolls during the same period: these are all around the area of the main village of Kentish Town. And then, in 1528, comes a very precise reference to an Ive family house which had another house nearby called 'le little Place' with the storehouse formerly called 'le Oldechapell with two chambers and cellars'. We know from Woodhouse in c.1704 that the old chapel in his house was being used for storage, and we know from the 1727 plan noted above that the chapel had two

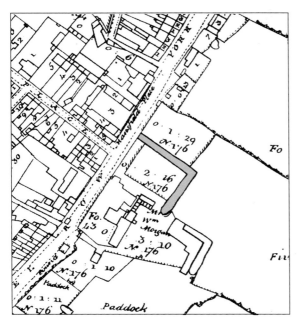

20. Extract from Thompson's map of St Pancras, c.1800. In the centre, extending south-east from the high street, is a stretch of water which then turns abruptly south-west. This has been shaded in this reproduction. South of this is Morgan's farmhouse.

chambers. This building, was on copyhold land and appears to be in the area south of today's Kentish Town underground station. Was Ive, therefore, in the centre of the village of Kentish Town, using Bruges' old chapel for storage?

This remains conjecture because, due to gaps in the records, there is no definite connecting link between Bruges and Ive as far as 'le Oldechapell' is concerned. But one feature supports the idea – the moat. The 1727 plan (ill. 18) shows two sides of a ditch going east from the highway and then turning south behind the house. That shape of water may also be clearly seen on the c.1800 map (see ill. 20): its line crosses today's Wolsey Mews and then goes south through the back gardens of Islip Street and Caversham Road. This seems to have been constructed specially to enclose a house and it is too far north to have been made for a house on the site of Morgan's farmhouse. So, if Bruges' house was here, it would probably have been in the grounds of Nos. 240-242 Kentish Town Road.

A WITCHHUNT

Mr Woodhouse in his journal tells a story which illuminates the superstitious spirit of the age, but also gives some quite unexpected information about St Pancras Workhouse. In 1703, he writes:

> "An old man living at the Castle Inn gave out that he was bewitched by one Osburn and his Wife living at a cottage in the fields (inoffensive people near 70 years of age). It was cried in all the neighbouring Parishes that they were to be tried by ducking on such a day, when, about noon, a great concourse of people to the number of 1000 appeared in the town. The officers of the parish had privately removed the poor old couple in the dead time of the night to the church, as a place of safety. The mob demanded these unhappy wretches at the workhouse, on being acquainted that they were not there, they pulled down the pales and walls, broke all the windows, and demolished a part of the house. After searching the chimnies and ceilings without effect they siezed the governor, hawled him down to the stream, and declared they would drown him and fire the whole village, unless they delivered these poor creatures into their hands. The mob ran up and down with straw in their hands, and were going to put their threat into execution had they not found the two unhappy persons, who were concealed in the vestry room near the chapel. They immediately siezed these miserable creatures, stripped them stark naked tied their thumbs to their toes and dragged them in this shameful manner to the stream now increased by the rains, and after much ducking and ill-usage the poor old woman was thrown quite naked on the bank, almost choaked with mud and expired in a few minutes, being kicked and beat with sticks even after she was dead and the poor man lied long danger-ously ill from the treatment he received. To add to their barbarity, they put the dead witch (as they called her) in bed with her husband and tied them together. The master of the workhouse, fearing the consequences to himself, it was who informed these wretches where these two poor old people were secreted."

An inquest at the Castle found a verdict of murder, and some of the assailants were tried and convicted. Thomas Wallis, the main instigator of the attack, was executed at the place of the murder, much against the wishes of the local population.

The stream referred to was probably the Fleet, and the church probably that of St Pancras, but the ref-erence to the chapel suggests that the couple were later hidden at Kentish Town Chapel. The work-house is a surprise, since in 1703 it predates the first known St Pancras Workhouse, established in 1731, and indeed predates the Workhouse Act of 1723, the first to generally encourage parishes to establish them.

21. The Fleet river near Gospel Oak, looking towards Highgate; watercolour painting by G.A. Fripp, 1852.

The River Fleet

The best known of London's 'lost rivers' is formed principally from two sources: one near the Vale of Health runs through the Hampstead Ponds and skirts Fleet Road on its way to Kentish Town; the other rises in the grounds of Kenwood House, flows through Highgate Ponds, crosses Highgate Road at Swains Lane, then recrosses further south and joins up with the Hampstead branch.

The name almost certainly derives from *'fleot'* the Old English word for inlet or creek, and was applied to the southern part of the river, which was navigable from the Thames up to Holborn. North of that it was sometimes called the Turnmill Brook (therefore Turnmill Street in Farringdon), Holebourne and further north still the River of Wells – it is so described in a 1638 map (ill. 22) of its course through Kentish Town. Nowhere in the the Cantelowes Court Rolls does it have a name at all – it is always the 'ditch', though a sixteenth-century sketch plan of the Morant charity land in Kentish Town (see ill. 48) marks the river next to the 'four acre' field as the 'Fleete'.

The Hampstead and Highgate ponds were built at the end of the seventeenth century to harness the water supplies of the northern heights, in particular the two tributaries of the Fleet, to provide water for the northern part of the City of London. The ponds of Hampstead and Highgate were constructed by the 'Society of Hampstead Aqueducts', more commonly called the Hampstead Waterworks Company, as reservoirs. The water was brackish and never particularly drinkable, though expectations were lower in those days. In 1934, when the supply system was owned by the Metropolitan Water Board, the Fleet was used only to flush the Metropolitan Cattle Market in Islington. Millfield Cottage in Millfield Lane is the successor to the cottage occupied by the man in charge of the Highgate ponds in the eighteenth century. The name of that field implies the existence of a water mill at some time, powered by the Fleet, but no other field names are known which suggest such use of the stream elsewhere in Kentish Town.

From Highgate Ponds the Fleet flowed to Swains Lane, where there was a small pond on the site of the western group of shops. Further east it formed into a fish pond at the junction of St Alban's Road and Brookfield Park – probably a contrived amenity by an owner of the mansion which faced Highgate Road here (see pp. 36-37) – then went south-east as the boundary of the grounds of today's La Sainte Union Convent and the southern edge of the Mansfield Bowling Club. It then formed another large pond on the west side of York Rise where it backs on to Twisden Road. Curving down through St John's College land it emerged at Highgate Road, just as Burghley Road does today, at Handford or Kentish

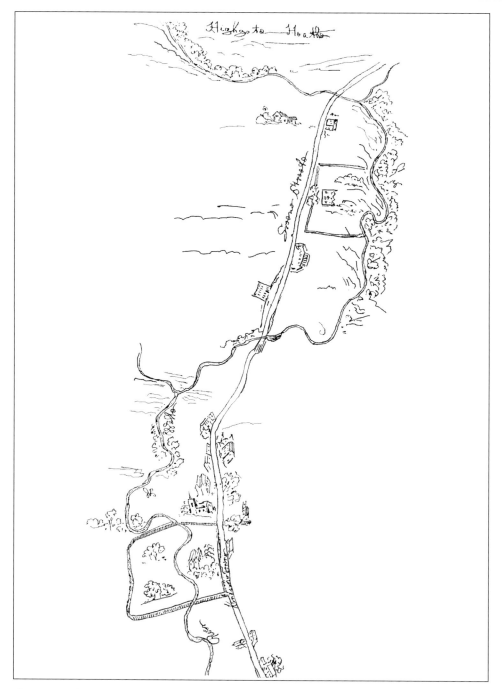

22. *Extract from a map of the 'River of Wells' drawn by 'J.E.' in 1638, contained in the Heal Collection. At the very top of the map, the river crosses Highgate Road at Swains Lane. Four large houses are shown south of this before the river once again crosses the road at today's Burghley Road. Two face each other at the top, one of which is on the site of St Alban's Villas or La Sainte Union Convent. The next house south appears to be in the area of Grove Terrace and below that is probably what became St John's Farmhouse, where Denyer House now stands. Kentish Town Chapel is shown west of the road further south.*

23. Bridge House, Highgate Road, in 1989.

Town Bridge – a residence called Bridge House stood here until recent years. At this point the river could sometimes be 13 feet wide. It then crossed beneath Highgate Road into the present-day hinterland of railway land.

It is beneath the new commercial centre opposite Kentish Town station that the Highgate Fleet and the Hampstead branch join. They do not merge, as some authorities have it, by Hawley Road. Certainly there was a junction there but only of two bits of the same merged river which had gone their separate ways from Anglers Lane around a 20-acre field. From Hawley Road the river crossed beneath the southern end of Kentish Town Road (then called Water Lane, from the frequent inundations), formed a pond at the site of Camden Gardens, and then went on its way through east Camden Town to St Pancras Way.

The 1800 map of the parish shows the Fleet still above ground through Kentish Town and mostly well removed from houses, so that it is unlikely that it was then much used as a sewer. Apart from its probable use by the Holmes family in its tanning business, and a possible use by a brewery in the 1830s near where the two streams joined, the Fleet seems to have had no industrial use in Kentish Town. More ominous for the river was a memorial presented to St Pancras Vestry in 1862 from 59 influential residents in the neighbourhood of Grove Terrace complaining that the 'brook' at the rear now received the drainage from a large number of houses recently built. It was an important open sewer which, the Medical Officer of Health calculated, was used by 200 houses. There was a strong smell, he noted.

There were several bridges as it meandered through the area. One was just east of York Rise, where a footpath leading from the rear of the Bull & Last in Highgate Road crossed the river and went on its way to Highgate. That footpath marked the subsequent

division of back gardens between Croftdown and Woodsome Roads and it is not too fanciful to think that the line of trees that once enhanced the backs of those gardens were planted along that path to the river. Samuel Palmer in his history of St Pancras (1870) speaks of the Fleet overground at this point. "It is pleasant of a summer's evening to walk the meadow, or lean over the little bridge, and allow fancy to range back when that running rill flowed on to join the River of Wells pure and clear...."

Anglers Lane, right next to the river, was remembered by a man writing to a local newspaper in 1909:

> "The Anglers Lane of today connects Prince of Wales Road with Kentish Town road, and is, of course, a lane of brick and mortar. When I knew it as a boy it was one of the loveliest spots imaginable – so deserted in the early hours of the morning that, when the anglers were not there, some of the youngsters from the cottages around, and some who were not youngsters, used to bathe in the river.
>
> I passed through Anglers Lane some time ago, an aged man in a bathchair, and I found it hard to realise that my wheels were rolling their way over the Fleet river!"

The river is possibly the derivation of the place-name Kentish Town. The etymology of this is still not resolved. Kentish Town is not noted in the Domesday Book, the whole of the parish being listed under St Pancras. The earliest known spelling is *Kentisston* (1208) with subsequent variations, and in *c.*1235 it appears as *Cantisseton*, but generally the prefix is *Ken-*. Professor Ekwall in his *Dictionary of English Place Names* interprets this as being the '*tun*' of Kentish men. This supposed Kent connection is reinforced by the custom of land inheritance in the area (see p.15) called gavelkind, one particularly prevalent in Saxon and medieval Kent.

But F.W.M. Draper[1] in 1965 rejected this explanation. In his view Kent itself took its name from '*Cant*', meaning stream, and Kentish Town derived its name from the river that meandered through the village.

Cantelowes, the manor name, could have the same origin, but the first mention of it is not until 1321[2], some 72 years after the manor was possessed (1242-49) by a prebendary of St Paul's called Roger de Cantilupe. So, confusingly, the two names could have different origins. The suggestion that the manor was named after Cantilupe is supported by the fact that a Visitation of St Pancras parish made in 1250, just as Cantilupe ceased to be the prebendary, calls the manor 'Northbury'. For some reason – perhaps his foundation of the Kentish Town Chapel – Northbury may have been changed to Cantelowes soon afterwards in his honour. Kenwood, being part of Cantelowes and also one of the sources of the Fleet, could therefore have either as its derivation.

24. Kentish Town Chapel in Kentish Town Road, in the eighteenth century.

Kentish Town Chapel

The establishment of a chapel-of-ease in Kentish Town was, as we have seen (pp. 8-9) a more significant matter than a convenient means of avoiding trips to muddy St Pancras and to the parish church. It also confirmed Kentish Town's paramount position in the parish and, in effect, implied that it was the church that was misplaced.

Traditionally, the founding of the Chapel has been dated to the thirteenth century and credited to the Cantelupe family. Roger de Cantilupe was both prebendary of Cantelowes manor and vicar of St Pancras from 1242 to 1249. There is no evidence that this tradition is correct and a Visitation of the Old Church in 1251 gives no hint of a rival building to the north. But the next Visitation, in 1297, does, for it describes the old parish church as badly neglected. The faults are numerous: the churchyard required better fencing to keep animals out; the porch wanted roofing as did the nave; two windows were missing; water escaped from the font; there was no bier or pall for the dead poor; the chancel needed better roofing and the windows on the east side needed repair, and so on. Significantly also, the vicarage was in a ruinous state. All this indicates that the congregation had another building to spend its money on and that the vicar had an alternative residence.

We do not know where the thirteenth-century Kentish Town Chapel was. If it had been founded by Cantilupe no doubt he would have placed it on his own Cantelowes manor lands on the east side of Kentish Town Road. In discussing the location of William Bruges' house (see pp 23-26) note was made of an item in the Cantelowes Court Rolls of 1528 in which an Ive family house featured. They had another house nearby called 'le little Place' with 'the store-house formerly called "le Oldechapell" with two chambers and cellars'. The location of this 'Oldechapell', so far as may be judged from the court rolls, was in the area of Kentish Town Underground station. This building may perhaps be the original Kentish Town Chapel. The Ive connection is supportive, for in 1456, once a new chapel had been built on the *west* side of the road on land donated by Robert Warner, the Ive head of family at the time persisted in sitting in Warner's pew in the new building – a seat which presumably had pride of place. Was this because Ive had enjoyed the principal pew in a previous building (in his own house) and declined to be downgraded?

I suggested also on pp 25-26 that the Ive house and its various additions could have been the house of William Bruges, which we know *did* have a chapel.

Perhaps the Kentish Town residents were at first using the chapel in a house which Bruges had taken over (by 1416) instead of going to St Pancras church? This seems a bit far-fetched but not out of the question. There is also a curious coincidence of dates to be considered. Bruges made his will in 1449 (he died in 1450) and in this he left a good number of items which adorned his chapel to St George's church in Stamford. He did not bequeath his house to anyone, which suggests that it was to be sold on his death. In that very same year parishioners asked a prominent local landowner, Robert Warner, if they could buy some of his land on which to build a chapel for those who could not get to the parish church by reason of 'fould ways and great waters'. Could it be that the parishioners realised that the use of the Bruges chapel was coming to an end – perhaps he had told them of his intentions – and decided that another chapel must be found?

Warner had an acute awareness of what other people thought of him. He told the parishioners that he had bought the land only recently and if he resold it to them it might be thought that he needed the money. However, for the worship of God and the welfare of the parishioners, he gave them the ground, which he marked out with stakes, allowing space outside for processions. He also contributed £5 to its building costs and apparently supervised the building work. The site of that chapel is nos. 207-209 Kentish Town Road.

It must have been quite small. It was, according to William Woodhouse's journal, enlarged in 1633, but when in 1779 evidence was put forward to support the building of a replacement, even this 'enlarged' building was only 53 ft in length and 26ft in breadth. It was certainly in a bad condition by 1779. We learn that 'part of the wall bulged, the timbers rotted and broke, and the roof so much sunk that it hath been for some time propped and cramped and is dangerous for the inhabitants to attend divine service'. The chapel was demolished in 1784, the same year as the new one opened in Highgate Road. A 99-year lease of the building and its site was bought at auction for £150 by William Morgan who built another house there, using wainscotting from the church and gravestones for paving. This sale led to a court action

25. *The rebuilt Kentish Town Chapel in 1784. It has since been enlarged and refaced. The house on the left was later to be the home of Andrew Mensal, the headmaster of Gordon House Academy.*

in which the churchwardens (one of whom was the famous engraver Charles Grignion, who lived at 22 Grove Terrace) brought a suit against the vicar and the Church Lands Trustees for disposing of the building and site. In the event the site was recovered at the end of the lease, and in 1926 the freehold was sold to C & A Daniels, the drapers, so that they might fully develop their store if they wished.

The replacement chapel, designed by James Wyatt and consecrated in July 1784, was inadequate within sixty years, such had been the increase of population. A competition was launched for a new building but in the event the old building, then called the parish church of St John the Baptist, was reconstructed by the demolition of the east end and the building of a new frontage, designed by J. Hakewill. This was opened in 1845 and is substantially the church we see today. It was made redundant by the Church of England in 1993, stood empty until occupied by a group of ecological activists, and at the time of writing is used by the Christ Apostolic Church UK.

A Gentleman's Retreat

Kentish Town was not unusual in the eighteenth century in attracting City people intent on a country house. London was awash with trade and money from overseas adventures; joint stock companies abounded; builders and developers were making money on the capital's expansion. It was both a mark of prestige and of comfort to have a summer house away from the pollution and the smells of the City, and Londoners looked to villages like Hackney, Hampstead, Fulham, Norwood, Camberwell, Highgate and Ealing. Highgate was already established in this way in the seventeenth century – a number of quite grand houses were built on the northern heights on both the St Pancras and Hornsey sides of the High Street.

Kentish Town, the Cantelowes court rolls show, had for long contained a smattering of 'Citizens of London' owning property in the area, but not always living in the houses they inherited. It was, no doubt, a place for a peaceful retirement. Indeed, Mr Woodhouse right at the beginning of the century noted that the village had 'some very fair houses, the residents are retired Citizens and others of moderate

fortune the branches of noble families." But by 1775, when Walter Harrison published his history of London, the settlement of Kentish Town was a more positive matter. He notes that Kentish Town was "formerly a very small village, but is now very considerable; for the air being exceedingly wholesome, many of the citizens of London have built houses in it; and such whose circumstances will not admit of that expense, take ready-furnished lodgings for the summer, particularly those who are afflicted with consumptions and other disorders. Here are several boarding schools and many public houses, it being much resorted to, especially in summer time, by the inhabitants of London."

The village did not achieve the social status of Chelsea, Kensington, Hampstead or Greenwich – it lacked the Thames, royalty and a spa – but its nearness to London and its undoubted rural beauty made up for much of that.

DR STUKELEY

One man who settled here was Dr William Stukeley (1687-1765), archaeologist, antiquary and clergyman. He was rector of St George the Martyr, Queen Square, but felt thoroughly at home in Kentish Town which was "extremely convenient for keeping my horses

27. Stukeley's own plan of his farm yard at Kentish Town.

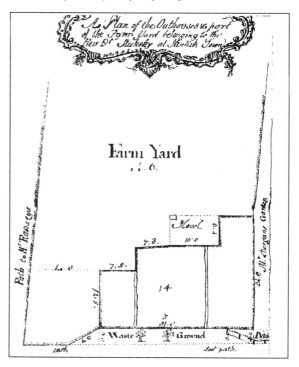

26. Dr William Stukeley.

28. *The view of KentishTown Road opposite Stukeley's house.*

and for my own amusement ... an half-hour's walk over sweet fields [from his church]. 'Tis absolutely and clearly out of the influence of the London smoak, a dry gravelly soil, and air remarkably wholesome." Mary Shelley, who stayed briefly in roughly the same spot as Stukeley, but over sixty years later, denounced Kentish Town as an "odious swamp". He named another advantage: "... exceedingly soft and good water from the springs at the bottom of the sandy part of Hampstead Heath under Caen Wood. 'Tis brought in pipes to our doors, and by my contrivances makes a little river through my garden."

Stukeley took over the lease of a house in 1759 from Samuel Hoggins, licensee of the Castle Inn, on land owned by St Bartholomew's Hospital. Most probably this was in Kentish Town Road, facing what is to-day's Prince of Wales Road. In 1760 he acquired on lease a second cottage there with additional land for £600 and despite his age began enlarging the property and extensively cultivating the garden. He added a bed chamber, built a 'Druid Walk' and an 'Eve's bower', and installed his own mausoleum decorated with family pictures and a bust of Cicero. In the garden he planted 230 crocuses as well as many unusual plants.

Stukeley was keen on the archaeology of the area. He conducted friends – who included the Lord Chief Justice and Martin Folkes, President of the Royal Society (see p. 20) – over the terrain near St Pancras Old Church, where he conjectured that a Roman camp had been established. He erred in this, and also in assuring people that the Castle Inn was once the Cantelowes manor house (another one!). The latter he was certainly wrong about, since the inn was in Tottenhall manor. Much of his work was not well-founded, but to the practice of archaeology, which was then in its infancy, he brought enthusiasm and knowledge.

By an odd coincidence Stukeley rescued from St George's church, Stamford, a window depicting William Bruges (see p. 23) that had been removed along with others because the stained windows made the church too dark. Stukeley, who hated to see ancient objects thrown away, installed it in his own house in Kentish Town. Most likely that window had been erected in memory of Bruges because he left a good many items from his chapel in Kentish Town to St George's, the parish church of a town which was probably his birth place.

THE FARM LANDS AROUND

Settlers or no, Kentish Town's economy revolved around agriculture during the eighteenth century. The demands of a growing London ensured a gradual change from pastoral farming to haycrops – the horses had to be fed. This is illustrated in the records of Christ Church, Oxford who let their Kentish Town Farm (Caversham Road/Islip and Gaisford Streets) to William Morgan. In 1795 the College's agent noted that 'By the tenant's lease the farm is considered a cow farm, and the tenant has covenanted to consume the hay on the premises and spread the dung on the land. The reverse has been the practice and he wishes to sell the hay in London and bring back dung as he is too far from London to sell his milk to advantage."

Another large farmhouse was that belonging to the St John's College estate. This building, which still remained in 1867 but then used as a school, was on the site of Denyer House, Highgate Road, just beyond the railway bridge. It was depicted by James King on his Kentish Town Panorama (ill. 29), when it was occupied by William Minshull, "a county magistrate of high respectability". St John's College, Cambridge had been the fortunate recipient of land bequeathed to it by William Platt in 1637, and when it was developed in the nineteenth century notables asso-

30. *Another view of Morgan's Farm, on the east side of Kentish Town Road. (See also ill. 2). From King's Panorama.*

ciated with the College, such as Lady Somerset and Roger Ascham, were used for street names but, ungratefully, Platt was not remembered.

Almost opposite was another farm where the Mortimer family cultivated land owned by Lord Southampton, the lord of Tottenhall manor. His estate extended all the way up Tottenham Court Road (in parts on both sides), and then west of

29. *St John's Farm, Highgate Road, on the site of Denyer House.*

31. *A group of buildings on the west side of Highgate Road, just below Gordon House Road. They include the premises of Bush, the local carpenter, and the Mortimer family farm, numbered 39 on James King's Panorama. No 37 is today's Carrol Place, which has been rebuilt as part of a modern housing development.*

Hampstead Road, Camden High Street and Kentish Town Road up to Highgate. As with Cantelowes, Tottenhall manor had been in the hands of St Paul's Cathedral until the Dissolution. It fell to the Crown and then into lay hands, until in the 1760s it was acquired by Charles Fitzroy, later created Baron Southampton.

The Holmes family farm was off Kentish Town Road – its general location now marked by Holmes Road. This area in the eighteenth century became the first industrial part of Kentish Town for the river Fleet, which ran through it, supported the tanning activities of the Holmes family – a tanning pit is seen on the *c*.1800 map on the site of the Royal Mail depot. The smells from this, one of the most noxious of trades, could not have made the Holmes family popular, nor could the development of some of their fields later in the century for brick production.

Some fields had a temporary use in the 1730s when a horse-racing course was opened on St John's College land, on the site of today's Burghley and Lady Margaret Roads. It was bounded by College Lane on the west and the Fleet river on the east, and could be reached by a footpath running beside the White Horse public house. The track was opened by John Wiblin, both a carpenter and proprietor of the White Horse (the forerunner of the Vine), from which two coaches a day went into London. Wiblin's venture, 'Green Street Races', began in 1733 and was still being advertised in 1739. The present Vine building,*c*.1899,

is Tudorised, for all the world a successor to an Elizabethan inn. However, the White Horse, its antecedent, began in about 1730 and was the first pub on the site.

NEW BUILDING

It was not until the 1780s that building along this road began in earnest. The eastern side of Highgate Road was particularly affected. Just below Swains Lane a Palladian mansion was built *c*.1777. Kentish Town House, as it was called, is shown in two very different illustrations, 32 and 33. The first is of 1787 looking up to Highgate with West Hill on the left. The house shown on King's Panorama is substantially larger and since Mr King drew his picture before the house was demolished, presumably it is accurate. At some stage therefore the house was considerably increased in size, and as the rateable value remained unchanged in the nineteenth century until its demolition one suspects that this enlargement took place during the occupancy in the late eighteenth century of Robert Milligan, promoter of the West India Docks[1]. The house lay back from the main road, with a pond fed by the river Fleet to the rear. It is supposed to have been modelled on Wanstead House in east London – it does indeed have similarities, but Wanstead House is much larger still.

The man who provided the money for the first building was Gregory Bateman, a London solicitor,

32. *Kentish Town House, Highgate Road in the later eighteenth century. Highgate West Hill is to the left.*

33. *Kentish Town House as depicted by King in his Panorama in the nineteenth century. If King's drawing is accurate, the house has grown considerably.*

who also dealt in property in Covent Garden – at one time he owned the house, no. 31 King Street, in which Thomas Arne, the composer, had spent part of his boyhood. Why Kentish Town House was modelled on Wanstead House is not clear. An exhaustive search into Mr Bateman's life and career[2] has revealed only tenuous clues. Bateman, as has been mentioned, had strong connections with Covent Garden, where Inigo Jones's Palladian church dominates the Piazza. That church was restored in 1788 by Thomas Hardwick, the architect of Wanstead's classical parish church, built 1787-90.

King in his Panorama asserts that Bateman was "ruined" by the expenditure. If he were bankrupted he would normally have been struck off as a solicitor, but he was still practising law in 1797. However, he had surrendered the house by 1783 to bankers in the Strand, perhaps on a mortgage to tide him over, and by 1792 we know of another tenant in the house. In 1819 the house was sold to Philip Hurd, a rich lawyer of the Inner Temple and it was demolished *c.*1850, when St Alban's Villas and St Alban's Road were laid out. (The Villas once extended to the Duke of St Alban's public house, but that end of them was bombed in the last war.)

At about the same time as Bateman was building his 'folly', further down the road Grove Terrace was being constructed. This was facilitated when the Dartmouth Estate, whose fields occupied the land

34. The construction of Grove Terrace, as depicted on King's Panorama. Miss Browell's school is in the building on the left.

behind, obtained permission to enclose the common land fronting the highway in 1772 (it was eventually bought by St Pancras Council in 1903). The developer of the terrace was thus able to provide rights of way to the main road. The first houses, at the northern end, were complete by 1780. They were built and owned by John Cheeke, a carpenter of Drury Lane, who also later owned the Bull & Last. Cheeke died in 1794, the terrace still incomplete. His widow married Richard Cooke, a stonemason, who finished building this particularly striking group of houses.

Much of the rest of this side of the road down to the southern end of Kentish Town remained undeveloped in the eighteenth century. Little Green Street, with its small houses with bow windows, has amazingly survived the onslaught of the railway. The enclosure of its site was permitted in 1723 and most probably the houses were built from 1777, when the land was leased for 66 years to a mason and a carpenter. Little Green Street joins up with College Lane, an ancient right of way between the cultivated fields to the east and the common and waste bits of land that fronted the main highway. The lane today emerges in Woodsome Road to the north, but in the eighteenth century it continued to the rear of the Bull & Last, where it turned to the east, crossed the river Fleet (on the site of the Mansfield Bowling Club) and then went up to Highgate.

Bridge House at 58 Highgate Road was demolished in 1989 and its site is now taken for flats built by an Irish housing association. Its garden ran south down to a pond at the junction with today's Burghley Road and the crossing of the Fleet beneath Highgate Road, a spot known as Handford Bridge in the manor court records. South of today's fire station was Willow Walk, a handsome group of houses around a squarish paddock. The northern side of this is today's Fortess Walk, where one house with a mansard roof, on the corner with Fortess Road, appears to be a survivor from an earlier period, but the rest

35. Willow Walk was a group of houses surrounding a paddock, roughly on the site of the present Tally-ho pub and the lower end of Fortess Road. The houses were occupied by professional people, including one of the village physicians. Today's Fortess Walk corresponds with the pathway to the left of the picture. From King's Panorama.

36. Village House, Kentish Town Road, is to the extreme left. The house is still there, but with a pale green glass extension in front of it, used by an estate agent. It faces south, just by Leverton Place.

went with the construction of Fortess Road.

Close to the Assembly House was and is Village House, now identified as no. 304 Kentish Town Road. It is hemmed in by other buildings and has a modern glass extension to its front housing an estate agent. This hides the typical early eighteenth-century form of the house, but a new owner in 1985 restored its twelve-paned windows and some interior features. It achieved some notoriety in 1818 when the occupier, a Captain Borthwick, advertised himself as a tutor of music to young women. It was found by one mother, who had put her daughter there, that there were no other pupils and Borthwick's intentions in regard to her daughter were nothing to do with music.[3]

The Assembly House was one of the principal inns of the village. As we have seen (p. 19) it changed its name from the Bull, or Black Bull in 1784, when the new Kentish Town Chapel was built nearly opposite, at the zenith of Kentish Town's social fortunes. It stood to the rear of the present ornate building and had extensive gardens where in 1783 there was trap-ball, skittles and a summerhouse. A year later, however, the proprietor, Thomas Wood, was falsely accused of highway robbery and after incarceration in Newgate prison went 'raving mad', a condition probably brought on by epilepsy. Older customers of the present building will remember a marble-topped table that used to be there around

which was inscribed in Latin a statement that testified to Robert Wright's return to good health in 1725. This was made, it seems, on the instructions of a man who had convinced himself that his walk there each morning for breakfast had saved his life.

South of this not much development occurred on this side of the road, all of which was owned by Christ Church, St Bartholomew's Hospital and the Dartmouth family. Proper development, as opposed to the haphazard construction of buildings on the waste, was, however, happening on the other side of the road in the late eighteenth century. Old Chapel Row, named after Kentish Town Chapel which had been sold off, was built from Anglers Lane to Holmes Road, and then another, and very regular terrace, York Place, went north from there. New Chapel Place was built at the turn of the century opposite the Assembly House.

By the end of the eighteenth century Kentish Town was a town rather than a village. A London street directory of 1799 lists (probably incompletely) a number of shops and suppliers in Kentish Town. It included two shoemakers, a cornchandler, a baker, a haberdasher and one general shop. Other skills available were supplied by a wheelwright, coachmaker, farrier, stonemason and a cooper. A number of farriers and blacksmiths are noted in the court rolls and we know of Morgan the blacksmith, only because when his wife died in 1764 a £1,000 note was

37. Eighteenth-century Kentish Town – asses milk sold in the street.

38. *Old Chapel Row in the nineteenth century. It was developed near the site of the old Kentish Town Chapel.*

39. *Ravenswood, one of the attractive late eighteenth or early nineteenth century houses in The Grove, opposite Grove Terrace.*

40. *The Limes, in The Grove, Highgate Road. This photograph was taken in 1910.*

found concealed by her in a drawer, without her husband's knowlege – this was a time when the wife's possessions were automatically those of her husband.[4] A farrier was in business at the top of Royal College Street until the 'model dwellings' were built at the apex of that street and Kentish Town Road. The nearby road, Farrier Street, is named after him. No doubt there were also many itinerant tradesmen, such as the seller of meat 'up and down Kentish Town' noted in the parish registers in 1702, and the establishment selling asses milk on the street, shown in illustration 37.

A DARKER SIDE

For people like Stukeley, Kentish Town was a peaceful place to potter about in. And yet it had its darker side. Highway robbery was particularly prevalent in mid-century and ample newspaper cuttings exist in the Heal Collection relating to incidents in the Kentish Town area. One of 1761 notes that five robberies between Kentish Town and Highgate were committed by the same man on the same day. Kentish Town was not unusual in this respect – the roads into London from all directions were infested with robbers and many villages formed their own patrols to offset the dangers of night-time. In 1756 two armed men were paid by Kentish Town residents to escort people from the Assembly House to the Foundling Hospital in Bloomsbury and back, twice each evening in the winter. In 1763 a patrol went from the Bull & Last to Great Ormond Street at 7pm, returning at 8pm. The problem reduced with street lighting, the growth of population and the introduction of the police force, but that it still existed (unless he was extremely eccentric) is illustrated by the fact that Thomas Lea, a business man who lived in Highgate, drove to town each down in his phaeton taking with him two loaded pistols which he left at the Duke of St Alban's pub, at the foot of Highgate West Hill, on the way down, and collected on the way back.

In 1775 the Vestry noted the need for a building to 'contain disorderly persons'. This 'cage', as such temporary prisons were called, was built two years later in Kentish Town Road, near today's Caversham Road, where a pound in which stray cattle were placed already existed. The building cost £20 to erect. The following year the government proposed that a public gallows be established at what is now Camden Town Underground station, outside the workhouse. This plan was never carried out. It was by no means unusual in London to execute a criminal at the scene of the crime. This happened in Kentish Town in 1786, when Joseph Rickard, aged 17, convicted of the murder of William Horseman who lived next to the former Chapel in Kentish Town Road, was hanged in the road opposite his victim's house.

41. *The Gothic, the most northerly house in The Grove, Highgate Road. Its site is now taken by Parliament Hill School for Girls.*

42. *These houses stood in Montevideo Place, at the top of Royal College Street, opposite the Castle Inn. The roadway here, and the entrance to Kentish Town near the Castle, were both very narrow. They were widened and old buildings demolished in a scheme completed in 1886. Artisans' flats were built on both sides of Royal College Street, and Farrier Street, named after a local farrier's business, was constructed to connect the two main roads south of the apex.*

43. *'Colonel Jack Robbing Mrs Smith going to Kentish Town'. St Pancras Old Church may be seen in the distance.*

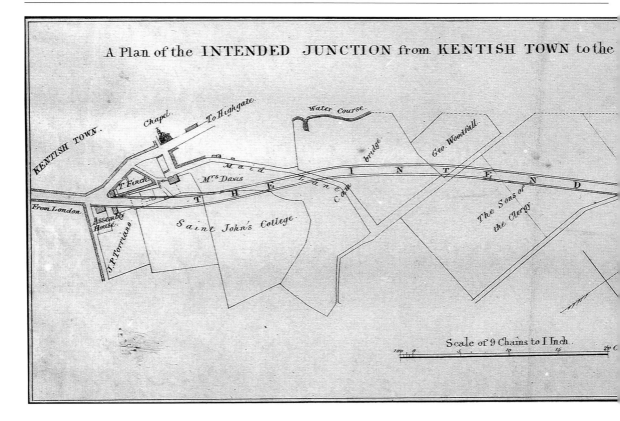

A Plan of the INTENDED JUNCTION from KENTISH TOWN to the

The Making of the Junction Road

It had always been a problem for Londoners to travel directly north, for the slopes of Highgate in particular were immensely difficult in the winter months. A laden horse going up the muddy slopes of Highgate Hill or Highgate West Hill was a reluctant horse. Circumventing Highgate the traveller encountered Hampstead or Muswell Hill, so little was gained by a diversion. In 1805 a serious proposal was made to construct a road across Parliament Hill Fields and Kenwood, using a dip in the terrain.

The problem was solved eventually by the creation of the Archway Road. It was called 'Archway' because the first plan, and one that got some way into construction, was an arched tunnel beneath the ridge of high land that ran from the backs of the houses in Highgate High Street over to Hornsey. Unfortunately, the tunnel collapsed in 1812 and a new scheme was attempted. In effect, the wedge of land behind the High Street was excavated away and a bridge

built to carry the old Hornsey Lane. It is difficult now to imagine such a large mass of land in this vicinity.

It was important to the promoters of this costly road that there was adequate access to it. Holloway Road and Upper Street served travellers from the City, but from the West End there was no good route. So at the same time as pushing its plan to build the Archway Road, the promoters filed at Quarter Sessions, as a preliminary to a Parliamentary Bill, a proposal for an 'Archway Union Road'. This was the beginning of the Fortess Road/Junction Road turnpike highway. Associated with these plans was the construction of New North Road, built eventually from Essex Road down to the City. All these projects were under the supervision of the engineer, Robert Vaizie.[1]

An optimistic prospectus was issued. It was a scheme "which cannot fail amply to remunerate those who may be desirous of embarking in the undertaking". The promoters' Act did not have an easy passage in 1811. St John's College opposed it for passing over its land and St Pancras Vestry had an interest too, since the route also passed over a piece of charity land called the Fortys or Forteys Field

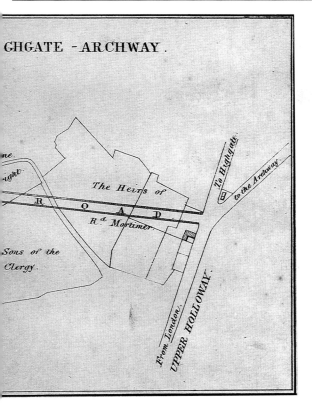

GHGATE - ARCHWAY.

The Heirs of

ROAD

R.ᵈ Mortimer.

Sons of the
Clergy.

To Highgate

to the Archway

From London.

UPPER HOLLOWAY.

(hence Fortess Road). But by 1814 the Vestry had settled with the promoters provided that there was no toll to be paid by foot passengers, and that no turnpike should be erected between the existing toll gate at what is now Tufnell Park Underground station and Kentish Town. Up as far as Lady Somerset Road the route followed an old path called Forteys Lane; beyond that it went through St John's College land.

Subscribers were impressed and the project was well funded. The road was probably opened in 1814 – a Vestry minute in April that year refers to it still as a 'proposed road'. But like Archway Road, it was not a financial success. It paid a 2.5% dividend (1% higher than Archway Road), and did even worse as the years went on. Reports of the Commissioners for the Improvement of the Road from London to Holyhead noted that Junction Road was in poor condition. In the 1860s it became the responsibility of public authorities.

44. A Plan of the Intended Junction from Kentish Town to the Line of the Highgate Archway'. The line of the intended road at the Kentish Town end was rather different when built. The Plan shows it beginning just by the Assembly House, whereas it was built slightly to the north. Also, the promoters appear to have redirected 'Maid' (Maiden) Lane so that instead of going up to Highgate as it now does as Dartmouth Park Hill, it joins Kentish Town near Kentish Town Chapel (St John's).

45. Fortess Road c.1905, near Tufnell Park Station.

46. *The main road through Kentish Town, up to Highgate, was controlled by a turnpike trust. A tollbar was erected by today's Caversham Road – it is shown above in this 1849 painting.*

47. *The tollbar was demolished in 1864. This drawing has been adapted from a contemporary photograph.*

Good Intentions

It was possible in 1863 for the splendidly named Samuel Wiswould to publish a book on the charitable foundations of the parish of St Pancras which ran to 128 pages.[1] Some of these concerned Kentish Town and at least three are still operative in some form or other.

JOHN MORANT

One of the earliest bequests to the poor of St Pancras is that of John Morant whose benefaction is noted in the first year of the reign of Edward VI – 1547 – though the bequest itself may have been earlier. Morant, we gather, was a Citizen of London, a member of the wool staple and one of the Merchant Adventurers of the Old Hanseatic towns and of Muscovy. The interest of the bequest lies not in what it did for the poor, though no doubt they were grateful for the

48. John Morant's charity lands in Kentish Town. West is at the top of the plan. To the bottom left are the fields eventually owned by the Christ Church Estate.

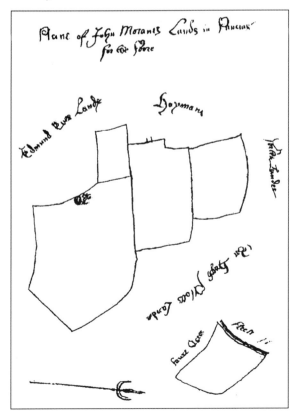

regular supply of loaves, but for the documentation that went with it. An old plan, almost certainly sixteenth-century, (ill. 48), copied by Ambrose Heal[1] and inserted into his collection of local material, shows land that Morant left to provide income for a priest and the poor. Wiswould in his book mentions only a gift of 4 acres which would provide a fund for the priest to chant an obit for Morant's soul at appropriate intervals, but he did not know or notice that Morant also gave 28 acres 'next unto Haymans'. The plan gives a number of clues as to the fields' whereabouts. The large field at the south, together with its extension to the west is clearly land eventually held by Christ Church – that shape, containing much of Caversham Road, Gaisford and Islip Streets, is evident even today in the street layout. The two contiguous fields to the north take in part of Leighton Road and its hinterland as far as Dunollie Road. The actual acreage does not tally, but the plan was drawn long before accurate surveying was usual.

The word 'Haymans' applies to land just north of Kentish Town station and 'Fortes Landes' to the Fortys estate through which Fortess Road now goes. In this rather out of scale plan we then have Sir Hugh Platt's lands – what became the St John's College estate, and the four acres, called Kilbornecroft, next to the Fleet river. In his bequest Morant actually says 'next unto the Horsepoole' On the c.1800 map there is indeed a field of nearly 4 acres by a pond formed by the Fleet in the right place. Today that field is the site of parts of Chetwynd Road and Spencer Rise.

In this plan is not only the first known map of any part of Kentish Town, but also the first naming of the Fleet river so high up in its course.

ELEANOR PALMER'S GIFT

The Fortys Field consisted of about three acres stretching north from Highgate Road in the direction of Tufnell Park. It is now divided by Fortess Road and the houses on either side are on the old charity's land. The origin of the name 'Fortys' is not known. It is not the only example in London – Fortis Green is at Muswell Hill, and east of the Tottenham Court Road was a 'Field of Forty Footsteps'.

In the sixteenth century Fortys Field was held by Eleanor Palmer, daughter of Henry VII's cofferer, who on her death in 1558 gave the land to charity; two thirds of the income was for the benefit of the poor of Chipping Barnet and one third for those of Kentish Town. Her death and her gift are inscribed on a plaque in Barnet parish church. Until the building of houses along Fortess Road the income was not substantial, and even then the Trustees had to wait for the renewal of leases to obtain a sensible sum. Before 1852 the income was distributed annually via the parish Directors of the Poor who were given tickets worth five shillings each for them to give out

49. *The first St Pancras Almshouses in Wilkin Street.*

50. *Poster advertising the election of a married couple to be inmates of St Pancras Almshouses in 1861.*

at their discretion. From that year the income was often used to support the work of the St Pancras Almshouses. Nowadays the revenue due to the poor of St Pancras is administered by the Fortys Field Housing Association, while in Chipping Barnet the Eleanor Palmer almshouses (successors to the ones erected in 1823) still stand, administered by the Eleanor Palmer Charity.

ST PANCRAS ALMSHOUSES AND THE GOVERNESSES

The St Pancras Almshouses were proposed by St Pancras churchwarden, Dr Donald Fraser, who with the support of other worthies raised £1500 in 1850 to buy a piece of land on the north side of what is now Wilkin Street, Kentish Town. The first almshouses, shown in illustration 49, were designed by James Colling, and had accommodation for about 100 people, either married or single, all over sixty years of age. It was a popular institution. Much financial support was gathered from regular special collections at local churches – the Archbishop of Canterbury himself preached at nearby Holy Trinity on their behalf in 1854, and in the same year a very large 'Fancy Fair', held at the Colosseum in Regent's Park, raised £200. But it was also in 1854 that the almshouses received some dreadful news.

The land they had bought was relatively open, part of the estate belonging to the Governesses Institution, of whom more anon. The Governesses held a rectan-

PARISH OF ST. PANCRAS, MIDDLESEX.

ELECTION (by the Directors of the Poor of the said Parish)
OF A
MARRIED COUPLE,
TO BE INMATES OF THE
St. Pancras Almshouses,
AS RECIPIENTS OF THE FORTESS FIELD CHARITY.

Notice is hereby given, that the Directors of the Poor will meet at

THE VESTRY HALL, KING'S ROAD,
PANCRAS ROAD.

On *TUESDAY NEXT, the 23rd day of APRIL, 1861,*
AT TWO O'CLOCK IN THE AFTERNOON,

For the purpose of receiving Applications (in writing) from Married Couples desirous of being elected Inmates of the Almshouses.

To be eligible for Election, Candidates must be over sixty years of age; have paid Rates and Taxes in St. Pancras for at least ten years; and never have received Parochial Relief.

The Letters of Application and Recommendations are to be addressed to me, and left at the Vestry Offices before Twelve o'clock on Tuesday next; and Candidates are to be in attendance at the Vestry Hall, at Three o'clock in the Afternoon of that day.

By order of the Directors of the Poor,

Vestry Offices, Pancras Road,
April 16th, 1861.
FRAS PLAW, Clerk.

N.B.—The Election will take place on TUESDAY, the 30th instant.

51. *A fete in aid of the Governesses' Institution in Kentish Town.*

52. *The Governesses' Asylum in Prince of Wales Road.*

gular site which stretched roughly from Weedington Road to Kentish Town Road. North and west of it development had already begun, and the Governesses had also permitted the construction of a terrace along the unused frontage of Prince of Wales Road. It was across this rectangle, in a north-south direction, that the Hampstead Junction Railway proposed in 1854 to build its line on viaducts to connect with the North London Railway. The line went obliquely across the almshouse buildings, but even then the railway company appealed against giving compensation equal to the cost of the whole group of buildings. The Court of Chancery agreed with the company – it need only pay compensation for the part of the group it proposed to destroy, but this absurd decision was overturned in a higher court.

The displacement by the railway, viewed retrospectively, was a blessing. The rest of the unbuilt area was, once the railway came at roof level, packed with the densest and worst of Kentish Town housing. The almshouses were fortunate to have the money to move out of an area that Charles Booth in his Poverty Map of London in 1889 coloured dark blue – just above his very worst category.

The Almshouses transferred to a site in Southampton Road where the present houses, designed by Henry Baker, were opened in 1860. They are still doing what they were built for, very much on a shoestring, but with the enthusiasm of some devoted friends.

The Governesses Institution was one of those organisations that Victorians loved to invent. The founders were quite explicit about their aims: "to raise the character of Governesses as a class, and thus to improve the tone of Female Education; to assist Governesses in making provision for their old age; and to assist in distress and age those Governesses whose exertions for their parents, or families, have prevented such a provision." These aims highlighted the then lack of employment for women who were not working class. There were few jobs they could do without slipping badly down the social scale. They could become governesses or companions if they found no spouse, but then they suffered the indignities that came from being neither servant nor family, sometimes ill-regarded by both. Often, for no fault of their own, they would leave a position under a cloud, the spurned object of one of the males in the house, and without a reference.

Not all of them had difficulties in their employment, but they *were* dependent, and when they reached old age had little to fall back on. So, in this Institution, the founders did what the Victorians liked best: they combined charity with education.

Their asylum in the Prince of Wales Road was principally to house aged governesses. It was built on a number of empty acres, but just as with the Almshouses, this peaceful existence was not to last

53. The Tailors' Almshouses in Prince of Wales Road, c.1905.

long. They too were troubled by the railway viaduct crossing their land, although their asylum building – still there today, with the initials of the Governesses Institution in scroll work on the gates – was some distance from the noise. But the area itself changed rapidly from the time they took up residence in 1849. Eventually the Institution began to run out of money and moved out to Chislehurst, happy to leave their land for profitable development. The Asylum building itself was taken by Miss Buss for her Camden School for Girls and more recently it has housed part of St Richard of Chichester School.

THE ORPHAN WORKING SCHOOL

West Kentish Town became a centre for good intentions. There were numerous missions among the worst of the housing, and at the western end of Prince of Wales Road were two large institutions. One was the Tailors' Almshouses, built 1837-42, which consisted of residences and a chapel, built of red brick and stone in the Gothic style, surrounded by about an acre and a half of garden. This was the gift of a Mr Shulz of Clifford Street, off Hanover Square, and it was for the support of aged tailors of every nation in the world, irrespective of creed, an unusually wide spectrum in an age which defined the recipients of charity very carefully indeed. These almshouses were situated on the eastern corner of the junction

with Queens Crescent and are now supplanted by the Council block called Penshurst.

A larger enterprise was the Orphan Working School which stood on sloping ground behind today's Maitland Park Estate. This enterprise had been founded in 1758 by gentlemen whose intention was not to educate the many orphan children stranded in London, but to teach them to work. Years elapsed before reading, writing and addition were included in the curriculum. In 1773 a building was erected in the City Road to cope with the increased numbers, but by the late 1830s, with the lease nearing its end, the governors of the charity cast around for a new site. They chose 12½ acres of Lord Southampton's land near Haverstock Hill and in 1841 bought them for about £5,500.

The brief to the architect included dormitories which had a bed for each child – not a common thing in those days in such institutions – with water closets nearby, and a dining room which could be used for religious services. It was, after a great deal of agonising over competition entries, designed by Alfred Ainger, who resigned near the end of the project after disagreement with the governors.[2]

The School, which opened in 1847, did not use all the land it had bought. Much of the remainder was developed for quite good class housing, which reflected its adjacency to Haverstock Hill, although the scheme suffered from the endemic bankruptcies of

54. The Orphan Working School in Maitland Park Road. The architect was Alfred Ainger.

55. *Mealtime at the Orphan Working School.*

builders. A Congregational chapel was erected on the south side of Maitland Park Road, and fronting Haverstock Hill a Presbyterian chapel was opened. The 'Maitland' name was used to honour the Maitland family, early and energetic patrons of the School during its City Road days.

THE CHURCH LANDS

In Gordon House Road, an old inscribed stone plaque has been inserted into the wall of one of Camden Council's less attractive blocks of flats. A hand on the plaque points to the Church Lands. In fact, there were four lots of church lands, all of them in Kentish Town, donated with the intention that income from them should support the parish church of St Pancras. The first we know of them is in 1189[3] but who donated them is not known.

The most northerly was an approximately 2½ acre field on either side of the junction of St Alban's and Croftdown Roads. This is now covered by between-the-wars Council blocks and the former Territorial Army Centre. Originally, the church held a field of nearly 4 acres that is now partly taken by the running track on Parliament Hill Fields, but this was exchanged with Lord Mansfield in 1875, when he owned the land from Kenwood to as far down as Mansfield Road, for a field of similar size further south. This fronts today's Mansfield Road and includes much of Roderick Road within its boundaries.

The third chunk of land contained fourteen acres. Some of it was subsequently developed as Dale Road and Vicars Road, but the rest was taken by the Midland Railway and was out of the public domain until Barrington Court and Kiln Place were built by the Council on surplus railway land. Lastly, a four acre field was to the west of Kentish Town Road. Again, much of it was taken for railway development and today Gillies Street and Arctic Street are the only roads built upon it. It is today land that can only be reached from Kentish Town by going along Spring Place, but the original access to it was from Highgate Road where a much longer Carkers Lane – that odd side-turning through warehouse buildings that still exists – went down to the River Fleet and to the church field.

56. *Ebenezer Maitland, an early supporter of the Orphan Working School.*

57. *Plaque pointing to the Church Lands, which is now inserted into a block of flats in Gordon House Road.*

Developing the Estates

The boundaries of the main estates in Kentish Town are evident in their architecture. The houses on the Christ Church Estate are different from those on the Bartholomew Estate; those on the St John's land, for all their variety, contrast with those on both the Dartmouth and Cholmondley land.

On a map of 1849 none of their fields is developed and off the main road hardly any building has occurred. There are some houses on both sides of Leighton Road, part of an estate of five fields stretching from the Assembly House to Brecknock Road, which at the end of the eighteenth century was owned by the exotically named Joshua Prole Torriano. Later family connections included Sir David Leighton of Charlton Kings in Gloucestershire, whose land agent was Prof. Thomas Leverton Donaldson. The street names today indicate the extent of this estate, which was substantially finished before adjoining estates were even begun.

The trustees of the Eleanor Palmer land had already capitalised on the fortuitous intrusion of the Fortess/Junction Road, and put houses on both sides of the road. Another substantial off-centre develop-ment consisted of ominously third-class houses, tightly packed into the area between Prince of Wales Road and Chalk Farm Road – it was not a good start for West Kentish Town. In this highly populated and very poor district the evangelical Rev. David Laing chose to erect a large church in Hartland Road, as part of the mission of St Pancras Church to serve a wider population. The land around here was developed in the usual terrace system by small-time builders, and there is little uniformity. The landlords, who included Sir Henry Hawley of Leybourne Grange and Lewis Buck of Hartland Abbey, themselves took little risk.

The Christ Church Estate, about 31 acres, was left by the Rev. Robert South of Caversham to his housekeeper, Mrs Margaret Hammond, in 1716 and upon her death (1735) to the College. William Morgan, the argumentative farmer who occupied the old farm house on the Christ Church Estate and also another across the road, moved out in 1831 saying that he was 'perfectly satisfied that to continue in it would be the means of my going to a gaol or a workhouse'. The Estate did not seek to keep him and two years later was considering plans for building on the Kentish Town Road frontage. They were having difficulties letting out the rest of the estate for building in 1854 because of 'war uncertainties' and it was not until the beginning of the 1860s that serious work began. One of the problems for Christ Church was that the land had no access to Camden Road and Lord

58. Caversham Road on the Christ Church Estate, c.1905.

Camden, whose land blocked the way, was less than co-operative. He had already built some houses fronting Camden Road and was disinclined to alter his plans to accommodate Christ Church. The result was that the exit to Camden Road from the Christ Church Estate is rather clumsy today (more so with the one-way system), because the only way was through Torriano land, via Busby Place and Torriano Avenue. At the end of Busby Place today is a large painted street name panel, making sure that we know the road leads to the streets on the Christ Church Estate. This emphasises the anxiety of the Estate that travellers would not know how to get into their newly built roads.

The St Pancras map of 1860 shows the roads of the Estate laid out with a church at the eastern end where St Luke's, Oseney Crescent now stands. A church was a necessary feature of any new large development, but here Christ Church was very lucky indeed, for they did not have to pay for the construction – they merely gave the site. St Luke's began as an iron church on the site of King's Cross Station, and in 1861 was a permanent building on the site of St Pancras Station. But not for long, because the Midland Railway, needing the land for its terminus, was happy to pay St Luke's compensation so that it could move elsewhere. The building was taken down and re-erected as a Congregational church in Wanstead, but it was decided to build a new St Luke's in Oseney Crescent. The architect was Basil Champneys, son

of the Vicar of St Pancras. This immediately suggests favouritism. No doubt there was, but at least Champneys was a good architect and the residents of the Christ Church estate got a good building – one that is now under threat from neglect. The church, built of red Suffolk brick, was consecrated on 4 December, 1869.

The Christ Church development was a mixed one. In 1865 it was noted that the houses on Kentish Town Road were occupied by tradesmen at £65 per annum, those in Frideswide Place by clerks in the City at £30, and those in Islip Street at £40-45. Caversham Road was 'highly respectable and let to solicitors, gentlemen and large tradesmen', but in Peckwater and Hammond Streets were poorer people at £25-33. About one third of the houses in Peckwater Street were occupied by single families, but the rest were sublet in separate rooms to whole families at 2s 6d to 3s 6d a week. No doubt rents and values varied in each street, for by 1863 the ubiquitous Midland Railway was obliged to pay £10,000 compensation for bringing in their line, at a sub-level, down to St Pancras. And in that same year another railway proposal, thankfully aborted, also threatened to divide the estate in two, but at surface level.

Adjoining Christ Church to the south was a part of the Dartmouth family holdings in Kentish Town. These twelve acres, developed in the 1860s, consisted mainly of Patshull Road, named from a family seat in Derbyshire. South of that was the estate bequeathed

59. Dartmouth Park Road, c.1905.

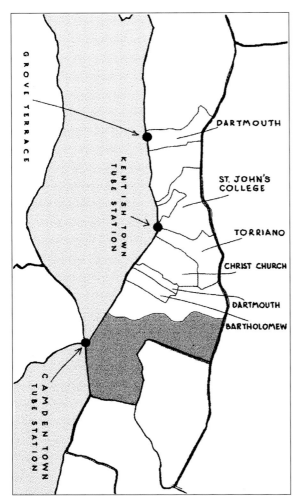

60. *Sketch map of Kentish Town area, showing some of the known estates.*

to the Hospital of St Bartholomew in the City by Thomas Cleave, haberdasher of London, in 1667. Part of it is taken up with Bartholomew Road and Villas, and the rest with one side of Lawford Road – John Eeles Lawford, who founded the Camden Town building firm of Lawford & Sons, was the land agent for the 5th Earl of Dartmouth.

Again, neither of these two small estates had access to Camden Road until Sandall Road was built in 1867 (Sandall is another Dartmouth estate connection). Eventually, to make matters easier for residents, Bartholomew Road was extended in a northerly direction right through to Leighton Road, so that the three estates were connected.

This was a busy time of building in Kentish Town for St John's College was also anxious to get some return from its farmlands. Development began with quite large houses in Burghley Road and Lady Margaret Road in the earlier 1860s, but by that time a good many substantial houses were on the market in the locality. The rest of the College's development was much more tightly packed. Roads built in the 1870s, such as Countess and Evangelist, represent a reduction of expectancy.

Off Highgate Road, another Dartmouth estate was begun in the 1860s. The first signs of Dartmouth Park Road appear on the 1860 map, a spacious development grandly climbing the slope to Dartmouth Park Hill. But apart from the construction of a few villa-type houses, it was the top end of the estate which was made up first with the much smaller houses of Churchill Road, Spencer Rise, Ingestre Road and the eastern end of Chetwynd Road, all deriving their names from Charles John Chetwynd, Lord Ingestre, who together with Lord Alfred Spencer Churchill, went into partnership as developers. The 1892 Stanford map of London shows these roads to be owned by the Conservative Land Society, one of a number of such societies formed during that period which wished to increase the number of people who could vote by fostering home ownership above a certain rateable value.

On the west side of Kentish Town Road and Highgate Road development was completely blighted by railways. It will be seen on pp. 81 just how much land was taken up with lines and depots, and most of what was left of the Southampton estate deteriorated so badly that it was targeted by the St Pancras House Improvement Society. Only on the very edge of the estate were good class houses built, such as those at the western end of Queens Crescent, and by the Orphan Working School on their land in Maitland Park Road.

Lord Southampton had, in fact, missed his chance in Kentish Town, where it became impossible to put up anything prestigious because of the railways. He

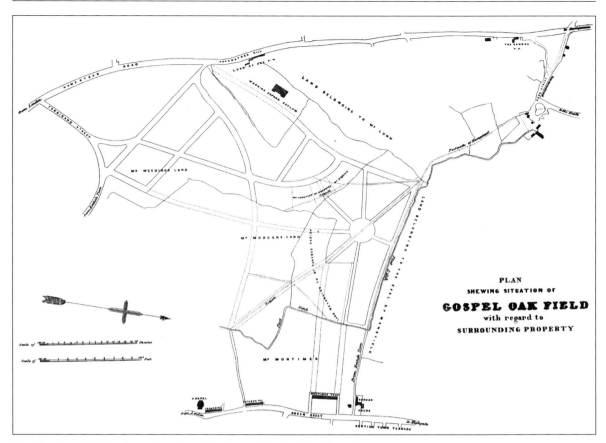

61. The Gospel Oak lands up for sale and development by Lord Southampton.

turned his attention instead to an area nearer to Hampstead. Gospel Oak derived its name from an oak tree at the boundary between the parishes of St Pancras and Hampstead, near Southampton Road. When the boundaries of the parish were perambulated every two years or so on Rogation Day, the procession of vicar, churchwardens, worthies and charity schoolchildren would stop at the oak tree and check that the boundary stone was still in place. It became the custom for the vicar to preach a sermon at this point. Perambulations took place well into the era when accurate maps were available and well after

the Vestry minutes had noted (1821) that the oak tree had gone.

The parish map of 1849 shows what became Lismore Circus laid out with other streets radiating like spokes. No houses are shown and by 1860 only Oak Village and a small number of other terraces had appeared. The truth was that the place was remote. Streets were not made up, the existing house stock was sub-standard and residents were at a distance from road transport. One suspects that Southampton wrote it off.

Schooldays

Not before time, the state intervened in the provision of education in 1870, when Forster's Education Act established elementary Board Schools. Previous governments had confined their role to subsidising the two religious organisations, the National Society and the British Society, in their efforts to provide rudimentary education for the poor and not-so-poor children of the community. But it was some time before the middle-classes and the lower middle-classes were persuaded to send their children to Board Schools which, from their inception, were perceived as being for the poorer classes. When the famous Frances Buss opened her second school for girls in Camden Town in 1871, one year after the Education Act was passed, her pupils came from mixed backgrounds – they were daughters of clergymen, builders, a boarding house keeper, a piano tuner, jeweller and an art dealer. There was a particular problem in the education of girls, for if their parents declined for social reasons to send them to National or British Schools, and after 1870 to Board Schools, the possibility was that the girls might not receive much education at all. Schooling did not come cheap on a piano tuner's earnings and though a son or sons might be afforded,

daughters had a lower priority. Numerous private schools continued to operate in every village around London after 1870, though most likely the education many provided was inferior to that in Board Schools.

PRIVATE SCHOOLS

Private schools came in all grades, from full-blown 'Academies' to simple one or two-class operations. At the end of the eighteenth century, there were five schools in Kentish Town listed in a London directory; in 1809 there were eight. It is likely that there were many more, located in houses where a semi-educated man or woman took in a few pupils, or an impoverished clergyman eked out a stipend.

The best known of Kentish Town's schools was the Gordon House Academy on the north corner of Gordon House Road and Highgate Road. It is shown by James King, himself a pupil, in his Panorama. Describing the building he says: "An old establish'd Academy kept by Mr. Cooper, who died suddenly of Apoplexy in the year 1788 whilst sitting at his Desk giving Lessons to his Pupils; among the number was the Artist of this Sketch. His Successor was A. Mensal, esqre, from Aberdeen, who married the Widow." What King doesn't say was that in 1841 he was Mensal's executor.[1]

It was Mr Mensal who gave the school its best

62. *Gordon House Academy, at the corner of Highgate Road and Gordon House Road. James King, the artist of this view, was himself a pupil in 1788 when the headmaster, a Mr Cooper, dropped dead during a lesson.*

63. *Southampton House Academy on Highgate Road. The house still stands, just beyond the railway bridge, converted into apartments.*

remembered name, but until very recently the reason for it was not known. A descendant of Mensal, Mrs Ann Currie, provided the answer: Andrew Mensal (1764-1841) was kinsman to the then Duke of Gordon. Mrs Currie's mother, Eliza Robinson had noted that "Andrew Mensal M.A. of King's College Aberdeen was born at Huntley in Scotland and was offered a living by the Duke of Gordon his kinsman. But he preferred to try his fortune in London whither he walked from Huntley barefooted knitting his stockings by the way; his grandfather, John Mensal, fought in 1745 at Culloden and his son James tenanted one of the Duke's farms."

By 1817 Mensal had retired and was living in one of the larger terrace houses now superseded by the Forum; later he is to be found opposite in a house now supplanted by the fire station. The Rev. Smith succeeded him and by 1832, another clergyman, the Rev. James Holloway was in charge. Holloway had some reputation as a preacher – he was minister at the Fitzroy Chapel in Maple Street. A family friend was Giles Redmayne, a mercer in the City, who at first lived with his family in a cottage just above Swains Lane and then, as wealth abounded, at the grand Winchester Hall on Highgate Hill. Redmayne's son, Robert, went to Gordon House Academy and each Sunday the family trekked off to Fitzrovia to hear Holloway's sermons.

The *Mechanic's Magazine* of November 1839 advertises the imminent opening of a College for Civil Engineers at Gordon House. It didn't stay long for, according to the rate books, it was gone by 1841 and is later to be found in Putney. Well before the end of the century the house was the residence of a succession of local doctors.

Nearby was the Southampton House Academy. Against all odds the building survives – the first building on the west of Highgate Road, north of the railway bridge. The word 'Academy' has been excised from the inscription on the facade, and the railway long ago took its playground, but it has been restored by Camden Council and converted into apartments – the Southampton Arms is next door, both buildings commemorating the fact that the land on this side of the road was part of the Southampton Estate. By 1828 (the house was built in 1820), it was being used as a school by John Bickerdike, who remained its headmaster until 1849.

Bickerdike's prospectus contained the usual form of mantra issued by such academies: 'His first wish for his pupils is that they should have the fear of God. He believes that from it springs in this life a self control and diligence, and dutiful and affectionate spirit, such as nothing else can give." He believed

64. *Rear view of Southampton House Academy during the headmastership of John Bickerdike. Much of the playground was later taken by the railway which crossed to the right of the picture.*

Clerk & Co lith: 202, High Holborn.

strongly in physical exercise, as well as education. He promised a sound knowledge of English, good spelling and grammar, together with Penmanship, History and Geography. All this for 24 guineas per annum, with an extra 4 guineas for drawing, engineering, architecture and surveying, and no charge for washing.

Other private schools operated nearby, one next to the Bull & Last facing south on to the gardens in front of Grove Terrace. This was Miss Browell's preparatory school, there by 1799. Almost opposite Southampton House was, also in 1799, according to King, "a French Academy kept by a Gentleman of the name of Jollie who, on the breaking out of the French Revolution in the year 1789 introduced the manual exercise and had his pupils regularly drilled and dressed in Uniform, all conducted in military order according to French nationality." The school did not thrive on its French connections – the house was empty in 1805, the year of the Battle of Trafalgar, and disappears from the rate books altogether in 1808.

NATIONAL, BRITISH AND BOARD

Before Board Schools were National and British Schools. The first National school in the area (so called from its administration by the National Society for the Education of the Poor in the Principles of the Established Church) was east of Royal College Street, just by its junction with St Pancras Way. In 1845 the vicar of St Pancras appealed to Christ Church College for a site for a new school, and by 1849 this was built. Its access road became Islip Street, for no roads existed on the estate at that time. The school remains today as the Kentish Town Church of England Primary School. The old school in Royal College Street became a laundry for some years, was rebuilt as a Board School and more recently has been part of St Richard of Chichester School.

The rival to the National School was the British School, administered by the British and Foreign School Society, mainly for the benefit of nonconformist families. Its building was 'rediscovered' by Gillian Tindall in 1980, substantially intact some yards back behind the facade of the Mornington Building Society at 158 Kentish Town Road, almost opposite Prince of Wales Road. The then manager of the Mornington remembered seeing the pillared and pedimented facade of the older building when it was briefly uncovered by workmen ten years earlier. The hammerbeam roof of the building was still visible.

The building began as an Independent Chapel in what was then called Trafalgar Place. It later became the home of the British School and the Kentish Town Literary Institution (see ill. 66). When the Mornington Building Society was founded in 1866 by local trades-

Kentish Town Parish

National Schools . . .

THESE National Schools (which are believed to be the oldest in St. Pancras) were flourishing a generation before the Board Schools were established, and it was in these Schools that many well-known inhabitants of the neighbourhood received their education.

The Government and Diocesan Inspectors invariably pronounce the teaching and work of these Schools to be excellent.

A Grand Bazaar

WEDNESDAY, 8th
THURSDAY, 9th } **JUNE, 1904.**
FRIDAY, 10th

At the Schools, Islip Street, N.W.

OPEN First Day, 3 p.m.; Second and Third Days, 3.30 p.m.   CLOSE each Day 10 p.m.

Prices of Admission

WEDNESDAY: 3 p.m. to 6 p.m., **1/-**; 6 p.m. to 10 p.m., **6d.**
THURSDAY : 3.30 p.m. to 6 p.m., **6d.**; 6 p.m. to 10 p.m., **3d.**
FRIDAY: 3.30 p.m. to 6 p.m., **3d.**; 6 p.m. to 10 p.m., **Free.**

Object

To procure Funds wherewith to liquidate the existing Debt on these Schools, and carry out the extensive repairs required by the Educational Authorities.

65. *Advertisement for a bazaar in support of the National Schools in Islip Street, 1904.*

66. *The British School in Kentish Town Road which, together with the Kentish Town Literary Institution, occupied an old Congregational Chapel.*

men, they held their meetings here in the building they were later to occupy as offices.[2] The British School continued to function well into the twentieth century, when it became a London County Council school. This appears to have closed by the First World War.

By 1871 the population of St Pancras was over 221,000, more than that of Camden today. Most were poor, many of them children, and once the London School Board had organised its resources the parish was a favoured area for its large, impressive but occasionally spartan buildings. In Kentish Town, Haverstock Hill, Hawley Crescent and Holmes Road Board Schools were opened in 1874. They were followed by Burghley Road and Carltoun Street (1884), and Rhyl Street and Fortess Road in 1898.

E.R. Robson, architect to the London School Board, writing in the *Art Journal* in 1881, justified the design of his schools, and the expense of them. Because, he said, they contrasted with the desperate poverty of the children's homes, they exercised a "sort of leavening influence". He went on: "The working man also appears quite to consider the schools in the light of a property peculiarly his own of which he may be proud, and not as an alien institution forced upon him by those of a superior station...They are simply common schools for the common people of the present time."

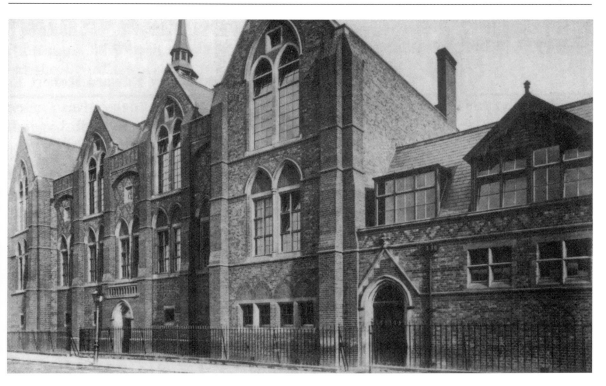

67. *Holmes Road Board School.*

68. *An al fresco class at Torriano School in the 1950s. The building was erected by the London School Board.*

Mansfield Road, Gospel Oak N. W.

69. *Gospel Oak School in Mansfield Road, c.1905. The building was bombed in the last war.*

The provision of pianos in Board Schools provoked a 'disgusted' letter in the *Hampstead & Highgate Express* in July 1890:

"I am sure that many thousands of hardworking ratepayers will learn with disgust the latest burden that is to be imposed on them by the School Board. By a small majority the L.S.B. has decided in favour of the introduction of pianos into its schools. Can nothing be done to stay this senseless expenditure?

Not only is the School Board the greatest imposition that was ever perpetrated on the public by forcing the reluctant and already over-taxed ratepayer to educate other people's children to, perhaps, the detriment of their own, but we are made to have this monstrous imposition forced upon us. It almost enables one to predict that the ratepayers will be asked next to feed and clothe the children.

It would be far better to teach the girls their duties how to make good servants and housewives according to their social positions than to have instilled into their minds ideas far beyond them."

THE SCHOOLS OF INDIVIDUALISTS

In the meantime two important schools had been set up privately. The first was founded by William Ellis, a former marine insurer. Born in 1800 of Huguenot descent (De Vezian was the family name, dropped during the wars with the French), he lived in the Regent's Park area until his death in 1881. Ten schools, known collectively as Birkbeck Schools in honour of the educationalist, George Birkbeck, owed their foundation to Ellis, though only one of them, the school in Highgate Road, survives today. He established what was called Gospel Oak Schools in October 1862 in Rochford Street, off Lismore Circus, but two years later the site was acquired by the Midland Railway for their line and the school then moved to Allcroft Road, where the accommodation was for 700-800 pupils. The basis for Ellis's method of teaching was that pupils thought for themselves – they did not rely on learning by rote. Needing more accommodation, William Ellis School moved to Highgate Road in 1937 and their old building became the street lighting depot of St Pancras Council.

Frances Mary Buss, whom we have mentioned earlier, is one of the foremost names in the history of education for women. She founded the North London Collegiate School for Girls in Camden Street,

70. *Gospel Oak Schools, later William Ellis School, in Allcroft Road.*

and then another school which became the Camden School for Girls. Needing more room, and with funding from the Clothworkers' Company, she took over the premises of the Governesses Institution in Prince of Wales Road, and after rebuilding opened a new school there in May 1878. It had a pleasant walled garden which contained a botanical area, and from there were still views up to Hampstead and Highgate. Miss Buss, it seemed, had two pet aversions – ink spots and wet feet, but she also imposed silence on her pupils and, one suspects, her staff.

The move to Prince of Wales Road occurred only a year before the earlier school, the North London Collegiate, moved to new premises in Sandall Road. (The North London moved out during the last war and the Camden School moved in to their buildings after bomb damage repairs.)

71. *Frances Mary Buss, founder of Camden School for Girls.*

72. An undated painting of the Castle Inn.

Inn Places

A list of public houses in the Sessions Rolls at the time of Edward VI notes one at Kentish Town and one at 'Grene Street' (Highgate Road). One suspects that there were more. In a Survey of the manor of Cantelowes in 1599, mention is made of a house called The Bull – an earlier name of the Assembly House; and in John Taylor's *Old Inns* (1636) there is a Rose Inn in Kentish Town kept by one, Gregory Machin. Justice of the Peace certificates were issued to seven alehouses in Kentish Town in 1634-5, though this may have included the St Pancras area. Cantelowes court rolls reveal a Whittington and his Cat in Kentish Town in 1712 – quite an early manifestation of the Whittington legend gathering strength and of the general belief that he was on his way up to Highgate before he was seduced back by the bells of London. And in 1721, when the craze for gin shops was prevalent, there are eleven Kentish Town public houses in the earliest surviving licensing records, some of which still trade.

The Castle at the entrance to the village is one of the oldest inns. The 1703 story of the witch hunt detailed on page 26 begins with a resident at the Castle, and when the building was taken down in 1849 a Tudor-style fireplace was revealed. The Castle stood back from the road at that time, on the present site of Castle Road, with a horse trough in front and gardens down to the Fleet river behind. An undated inventory (probably 1760s) notes that on the death of Samuel Hoggins, the landlord, the stock included twelve gallons of 'mountain sour wine', thirty bottles of Madeira, and 36 bottles of cyder. The total stock of drink and fittings was valued at £1145.

Next to the Castle, to its south, stood the residence of Thomas King, father of James King whose Panorama of Kentish Town has been so valuable. According to the artist (and others) it was formerly the home of William Suckling, Lord Nelson's uncle. It was often visited by the future admiral who "took much pleasure in Horticulture, and planted several Shrubs in the Garden, also some extraordinary box trees, preserved with great care by Mr. King [the artist's father], who experienced much satisfaction in shewing them to his friends." Mr King senior was here by 1802 at the height of the great man's fame, and is unlikely to have invented the story.

The Bull & Gate and the Bull & Last are both on the 1721 list. A St Pancras historian thought that the Bull & Gate was a corruption of 'Boulogne Gate', a reference to Henry VIII's acquisition of Boulogne in 1544, but this seems a bit fanciful – there are plenty of Bull & Gate pub names around. The same historian[1] in 1874 noted that the old building had re-

73. *Extract from James King's Panorama, showing Thomas King's house to the left, and The Castle Inn. It will be noted that the latter, which the artist must have known well (it was not rebuilt until 1853) is very different from that depicted in illustration 72.*

74. *The old Bull & Gate. Beneath this drawing is the inscription: 'The Bull and Gate, Kentish Town it was opposite this House that Mr Suton and Squire Greenwood were robbed by W. Yates, H. Morris and B. Fink who after frightening the Village got clean off but where afterwards taken and Hung at Tyburn in Year 1730.'*

The Bull and Gate, Kentish Town. it was opposite this House that Mr Suton and Squire Greenwood were robbed by W. Yates. H. Morris. and B. Fink who after frightening the Village got clean off but where afterwards taken and Hung at Tyburn in Dec. 1730.

75. *The rebuilt Bull & Gate, Kentish Town in 1904, much as it is today.*

76. *The Assembly House, c.1853.*

77. *Another view of the Assembly House, then called The Flask. Beneath is the inscription: 'The Flask, Kentish Town. Thomas Theobalds was taken here in bed for the robbery at Squire Mathews. Near Highgate Church on the 13th Aug. 1731.'*

cently been taken down and records that "A splendid modern gin-palace now monopolises the space, and the scene is composed of departing and returning omnibuses, amidst glare and excitement unknown a hundred or even fifty years since."

The Assembly House, previously known as the Bull and, briefly as the Flask (ill. 77), was a major Kentish Town inn. Its pleasure grounds to the rear stretched towards today's Lady Somerset Road; these now contain the extensive community buildings in Leighton Road and the long back gardens of some of the houses on that side of the road. It has been suggested that the Bull & Last may be a sly dig at the Bull with 'Last' implying that it was the last pub before the hill up to Highgate. This was not the case, however, since a pub called the Cow & Hare was at the bottom of Highgate West Hill and predated the Bull & Last.

The first Kentish Town pub that travellers from the City came across was the Black Horse, whose successor survives today built into the artisans' dwellings at the top of Royal College Street. In the late 1860s it was run by a Mrs Faulkner, a 'singular character' who drank her gin and water after her dinner each day, and smoked a pipe of tobacco in her back parlour, in which a pig might frequently be seen as her companion.[2] Also on the 1721 list is what is now the Jolly Anglers. When the Vestry met there in 1725 it was called 'The Compleat Angler',

78. *A report in the Illustrated London News in 1849 of a 'Violent thunder-storm' in Kentish Town. "Here the lightning struck a remarkably fine old elm, which had long sheltered the tavern known as 'the Assembly Rooms'. Some of the larger limbs of the tree were struck to the ground, and nearly fell upon a man who was passing."*

when the names of new heroes, or new members of the royal family displaced old, generally agricultural names. Changing a pub name to mark a modern phenomenon or personage is legitimate – history is recorded in such ways, but the switch to meaningless brand names simply to accommodate a marketing brief debases the whole thing. One famous and unusual pub name has gone – the Mother Shipton. This pub at the junction of Malden Road and Prince of Wales Road, now the Fiddler's Elbow, recalls a woman of the sixteenth century who warned, as they were inclined to do in those days in a couplet, that:

"Before the good folk of this kingdom be undone
Shall Highgate Hill stand in the midst of London."

What well-informed landlord rescued this dire prediction from folk lore and decided to use it for his pub in a building development that was soon lapping at the foot of Highgate, we do not know. But Mother Shipton would be mollified at the failure of her prophecy by the fact that Highgate West Hill, called Highgate Hill in her day, is adjacent to some of the most closely protected open space in London.

82. Mother Shipton, a print published in 1797.

83. The Tally-ho pub, which now extends from Fortess Road to Highgate Road.

84. (above) The White Lion and Bell, as depicted by James King in his Panorama (see p.73).

85. (right) The Oxford Arms in Kentish Town Road, photographed before the Underground was built, in 1904.

Kentish Town People - 1805

The following, described as living in Kentish Town, are extracted from *Holden's Triennial Directory of London* tradesmen and residents for 1805:

TRADESMEN

Adams, William, circulating library, Chapel Place
Adams, haberdasher and milliner
Adams, James, taylor
Allen, Anthony, gardener, 8 Mansfield Street
Barclay, William, tin plate worker
Barenger, John, glazier and painter
Beechey, Miss, ladies boarding school, Chapel house
Bluck, J. artist, Mansfield Place
Browell, Miss, boarding school
Bull, Samuel, dealer in coals, Mansfield Place
Burch, Edward, librarian to the RA, Paynes Place
Bush, James, carpenter, Green Street
Butler, William, painter and glazier
Byard, John, watchmaker
Cannon, Thomas, classical academy, Mansfield Place
Cautell, William, carpenter and joiner
Cauckwell, E. haberdasher
Chitty, John, corn and coal merchant, Willow Walk
Clark, John, cowkeeper
Clarke, James, boot and shoemaker
Clarke, Miss, boarding school
Clarkson, Miss, preparatory school
Collins, George, taylor
Cocker, Robert, dealer in wine and brandy
Ellis, Mary, sadler
Englefield, the Assembly House
Fort, Thomas, victualler [Bull & Gate]
Gambee, William, carpenter and undertaker
Gill, John, plumber
Goodman, John, watch and clockmaker
Gough, John, grocer, Chapel Place
Hall, Susannah, mantua maker, Old Chapel Row
Hall, Henry, Nags Head
Halsted, Charles, Academy
Hanwell S & J, Grove House boarding school
Harrison, Thomas, Mansfield Arms, Mansfield Place
Holland, Joseph, butcher
Holmes, William, tanner, Mansfield Place
Howell, John, attorney
Jones & Taylor, tanners
Joyce, John, smith and farrier, 1 Camden Place
King, milliner
King, Thomas, accomptant
Lambut, Ann, preparatory school for children, 8 Lower Mansfield Place
Mellow, Thomas, shoemaker
Mental [sic] A.A.M. Gordon House Academy

Morecraft, Robert, The Angler
Morgan, William, farmer
Odams, William, coach master
Oliver, John, Bull and Last
Page, William, cabinet maker and undertaker, Chapel Path
Parker, James, engraver, Spring Place
Savell, Wiliam, carrier
Senior, William, baker
Salden, Mrs, Ladies Academy
Smart, Thomas, shopkeeper
Snuggs, S., carpenter and builder, Willow Walk
Tew, John, cowkeepr
Thurgood, Robert, baker
Wilson, Phillip, pork butcher
Wilson, Edward, butcher
Wood, Susannah & Co, grocers
Worgan, Thomas, music master, 28 Lower Mansfield Place
Worsdall, The Old Vine, Kentish Town Road.

RESIDENTS

Bagnall, Mrs Elizabeth, Old Chapel Row
Baker, Mr John, 11 Mansfield Place
Barker, William esq, Spring Place
Bates, Mr Thomas 2 Mansfield Place
Beck, Mr Andrew, 5 Prospect Place
Bentham, George, Grove
Bettett, Joseph
Birch, Miss P., Terrace
Bird, Mr Thomas, Haymans Row
Blake, Capt., Spring Place
Blanchard, Mr Charles, 2 Upper Craven Place
Blew, Mr John, Mansfield Place
Bolger, Mr Robert, 2 Lower Mansfield Place
Bon, Mr George, 6 Mansfield Place
Brailsford, William esq
Browell, Mr Henry, Grove
Brown, Mr Benjamin, Willow Walk
Brown, Mr Robert, 5 Mansfield Place
Brown, Mrs Mary, Terrace
Burchett, Mr James Robert, York Place
Butterfield, Mrs Elizabeth, 4 Mansfield Place
Byron, Mr Thomas 9 Mansfield Place
Campbell, John esq, Willow Walk
Carr, Mrs Martha, Willow Walk
Carrott, Mrs Elizabeth, Craven Place
Champneys, Rev. W.B.
Chawner, Mrs Ann
Christie, Mrs, Lodge
Clarke, William esq, Kentish Town
Clerke, Mrs Margaret, 12 Mansfield Place
Clulow, William esq
Colley, Mrs Mary, Paynes Place
Colley, Mr William, 1 Prospect Place
Collingwood, Mr Launcelot, 7 Mansfield Place
Cooke, Richard esq, Terrace
Cooper, Mr Thomas
Copland, Mr John

Cox, Mr Thomas, 10 York Place
Croker, Mr Hugh, Haymans Row
Cullum, Mr John, 3 York Place
Davies, Mrs Mary, Craven Place
Davis, Mr, Terrace
Divett esq
Dunn, Mr Edward
Dyne, Mr William, Terrace
Eade, Mr William Jonathan, Holmes Terrace
Eddison, Mr John, Terrace
Edgeley, Mrs, 13 Mansfield Place
Edwards Mr Edward, 1 York Place
Elam, Mr Thomas, Old Chapel Row
Elliott, Mr William, Old Chapel Row
Fell, Mrs Margaret, York Place
Felton, Mr William, Spring Place
Field, Mr, 12 York Place
Finch, Thomas esq, Old Chapel Row
Griffin, Miss Susanna, 7 Upper Craven Place
Grob, John Ernest esq
Haedy, Mr Christopher, 11 York Place
Hall, Mr George, 16 Lower Mansfield Place
Hares, Mrs, 14 Lower Mansfield Place
Hargrave, Mr William, Mansfield Place
Harpeley, Mr Matthew, 5 Mansfield Place
Hart, Mrs Sarah
Hawks, George esq
Hebberd, Mrs Mary, 17 Lower Mansfield Place
Hedges, Mrs Sarah, Willow Walk
Heeks, Mr Anker
Hemingway, Mrs David, 6 York Place
Jackson, George esq, Terrace
Jackson, Mr William, Terrace
Jacques, Mr John, 7 Lower Mansfield Place
Jones, Mrs Ann, Paynes Place
Jouret, Mr James
Kelly, Mr J.A.
Kidder, Mr Arthur, 6 Mansfield Place
Knapp, Mrs Leonora, 3 Camden Place
Knowles, Mr William, Terrace
Lane, Mrs Elizabeth
Langley, Mr Bartholomew, 6 Lower Mansfield Place
Latchford, Mr John, 7 York Place
Macpherson, Mr Day, Spring Place
Main, Mrs, 6 Upper Craven Place
Marshall, Mr Edward, Mansfield Place
Mason, Mrs Elizabeth, Mansfield Place
Mathers, Mrs Ann, Grove
Maurice, Mrs Sarah
May, Mrs Sarah, Spring Row
M'Gowen, Mr John, 4 Mansfield Place
Meyer, Mr George, Willow Walk
Milbourne, Mrs Sarah, Terrace
Miller, Mr Andrew, 9 Fitzroy Place
Mills, Mrs Mary, Haymans Row
Minshull, William esq
Moore, Mr D., Spring Place
Morgan, Mr James

Morris, Mr William, 6 Lower Mansfield Place
Morris, Mrs Sarah Margaret, 5 Fitzroy Place
Munden, Joseph esq
Neep, Mr C.
Noble, Mrs Ann, Old Chapel Row
Paget, Capt. John
Palmer, Mrs Mary
Parker, Mr William
Penaler, Mrs Jane, Haymans Row
Peyton, William esq, Grove
Philip, Mr William, Old Chapel Row
Phillips, Mr, Craven Place
Phipps, Mr Thomas, Grove
Pickett, Mrs Esther, 14 Mansfield Place
Price, Mr Edward, Grove
Priddle, Mr Thomas, Spring Row
Randall, William esq, Terrace
Randall, Mr James, Spring Row
Randall, Mr John, Craven Place
Remnant, Richard esq
Richardson, Mr John, Spring Place
Roberts, Mr William, 8 Fitzroy Place
Roberts, Mrs, 4 Prospect Place
Rose, John esq, Grove
Rowley, Dr William, Willow Walk
Sewell, Mr Samuel, 9 York Place
Sherington, Mr William, Willow Walk
Simpson, Mr Stephen, 7 Fitzroy Place
Simpson, Mr John, 1 Mansfield Place
Sims, Mr John, 1 Fitzroy Place
Sly, Mr John, 4 Lower Mansfield Place
Smith, John esq, Terrace
Stable, Mrs, Terrace
Stanger, James esq
Starkey, Mr William, 3 Mansfield Place
Stevenson, Mrs Mary
Stocoe, Mr Alexander, Terrace
Stones, William esq, Terrace
Talbot, Mrs Frances, Paynes Place
Tarrant, Mr John Thomas, 4 Lower Mansfield Place
Tate, Mr Robert, Craven Place
Thompson, Mr Berks, Holmes Terace
Thompson, Mr Thomas 7 Mansfield Place
Topham, Mr William, Spring Place
Walworth, Mrs Amey, Old Chapel Row
Warren, Mrs Helena, 3 Fitzroy Place
Weldon, Mr James, 2 York Place
White, Mrs Jane, 12 Mansfield Place
Whittingham, Mr Thomas, Old Chapel Row
Williamson, Mr John, Holmes Terrace
Wilson, Mr John, 6 Fitzroy Place
Wilson, Mr Francis, Craven Place
Winter, Mrs Ann, 11 Mansfield Place
Wood, Mr John, 4 York Place
Wood, Mrs A., Old Chapel Row
Woodward, Mr Richard, Craven Place
Yates, Mrs Elizabeth, Haymans Row

Mr King and his Panorama

In 1930, when such things could be had cheaply, a firm of auctioneers offered St Pancras Council some unique historical documents. They consisted of two pen and wash panoramic drawings, about 36 feet long in total, showing all the houses on either side of Highgate Road (from Swains Lane) and Kentish Town Road, and then down St Pancras Way to St Pancras Old Church. There was an additional roll illustrating that part of Kentish Town Road that goes south to the Mother Red Cap at Camden Town. The only section of main road in the area not depicted was the west side of St Pancras Way. These panoramas were offered for the price, as it was prosaically put in the Council minutes, of £1 a foot.

They were put up for sale by a Mrs Capper of Reigate, the granddaughter of the artist. She was probably related to the Capper family which once occupied a farmhouse on the site of Heal's furniture store in Tottenham Court Road. The artist was James Frederick King (1781-1855), a Kentish Town resident whose house (3 Montague Place) was on the site of the booking hall of the old Kentish Town station, next to the Underground station.

There is no doubt that King mixed with the wealthier tradesmen of Kentish Town and the professional classes. On his death certificate the prominent local businessman and estate agent, Joseph Salter (who helped to found Salter, Rex) is noted as the 'informant' of the death. The Salter family was living a few doors away when King moved into his house in Montague Place in 1837; Joseph Salter was to begin his career as a St Pancras Vestryman in 1866. King, as we have seen (p.60) was executor of the will of Andrew Mensal, former headmaster of the principal private school in Kentish Town. The *Survey of Lon-*

86. Montague Place and Inwood Place before the building of the Midland Railway and the London Underground stations. The Assembly House, before its end-of-century rebuilding, may be seen in the distance. Leighton Road intervenes, then Montague Place is the group of houses immediately south of it. James King lived at no. 3, though it is difficult to know which is his actual house, because the rate books record more houses in Montague Place than appear in this photograph. According to a contemporary map there were some premises to the rear, which may have been counted as Montague Place.

87. James King's depiction of the premises on the site of his own house. "On this very Spot a respectable Cornchandler lived, of the name of Sewel. To get to his parlour you ascended a Step Ladder, which was tastefully furnished in the old fashioned style. Under were deposited trusses of Hay and Straw, Corn, etc., and when the premises fell to decay they were purchased by a Mr. Evans [who built] thereon 6 houses. On the very Site of Mr. Sewel's House the artist of this sketch has resided for more than 20 years.

don[1] had King as an official at Somerset House between 1820 and 1830, and in 1851 King put himself down on the census form as a 'retired artist'. His own father, Thomas King, an 'accomptant', lived in a largish house just south of the Castle Inn by 1802, when the surviving rate books begin. Undoubtedly, the Kings were in Kentish Town well before this, because as James King notes in his commentary to the Panorama, he was actually in class at the Gordon House Academy when the former headmaster dropped dead in 1788, and a Thomas King is first recorded as a Surveyor of Highways for the northern part of the parish in the Vestry minutes of 1787.

The drawings on King's Panorama are clearly designed to show the Kentish Town area as it appeared in about 1800, though the commentary throws in information which relates to much later years. The question arises – were the drawings done in c.1800 (when the artist was about nineteen), or were they done later, perhaps redrawn from sketches done in boyhood and reassembled? Or else, were they done from memory? Part of the answer to this was found during the facsimile publication of the Panorama in 1986 by the London Topographical Society.[2] It was found that the watermarks of two of the rolls showed the dates 1848 and 1850.

With some notable exceptions, the Panorama matches pretty well the position of houses as shown on the authoritative map of the area made c.1800, though there are not enough contemporary illustrations of buildings to make a judgement as to the reliability of the front elevations. As it is unlikely that King, fifty years later, could have remembered the buildings and their positions, it has to be assumed that he made preliminary drawings over the years which he then revamped for his finished work. It is a notable achievement, for what we have is Kentish Town as a small town, with 'Green Street' (Highgate Road) still very much a village with the odd mansion, the little businesses that served an agricultural community, the tiny cottages that housed large families, and the pubs before they were rebuilt in the great Victorian pub-building boom. King also depicts the condition of the roads and lanes with examples of the traffic upon them.

James Frederick King died in January 1855 and was buried in Highgate Cemetery, where his tombstone is still decipherable. It would be nice to remember King with a plaque outside the old Kentish Town station, the site of his house, perhaps on the wall which overlooks the railway.

Divided by Lines

THE RAILWAY LANDS

Much of the railway land of Kentish Town is hidden, but illustration 88 reveals its hold on the topography of the place. The first intrusion on the southern fringes of Kentish Town was at rooftop level, when in 1850 the North London Line, primarily a route to move freight from the London North Western Railway depot at Camden Town to the docks at Blackwall, was opened. It mirrored the line of the Regent's Canal, the function of which some thirty years earlier was to convey freight from Paddington basin to Limehouse. The railway's route locally went from Caledonian Road station to Chalk Farm and the LNWR depots there. But in 1860 the Hampstead Junction Railway was built, which made a much more indelible impression on the area. It joined the North London just south of Hawley Road and then went north through West Kentish Town up to Gospel Oak (then called Kentish Town Station!) and on to Hampstead Heath. This is the route we now think

of today as the North London Line. Again, much of this was at roof top level, blighting the streets, already of poor quality, even further.

In 1868 the Tottenham and Hampstead Junction Railway came in from the east, locally from Holloway Road, beneath Junction Road (where there was a station) and then above Highgate Road, where there was a high level platform and a station exit on the west side of the road, to join the Hampstead Line very near Gospel Oak Station. A further development of this new line, in association with the Midland, had a low level platform at Highgate Road where the line went in a curve beneath the road to join the morass of Midland Railway tracks in the centre of the railway lands.

The Midland, with its terminus at St Pancras, came late into London (1863), and therefore caused the most damage. From St Pancras, it went beneath Agar Grove and Camden Road (where there was a station), through the Christ Church Estate at a low level, then beneath Highgate Road at Kentish Town Station and into the old farmland that had belonged to the Southampton family and which was the only suitable green field site left south of the land of Lord Mansfield.

88. A section of Bacon's map of London, 1882, showing the interconnnecting railways which divided east and west Kentish Town.

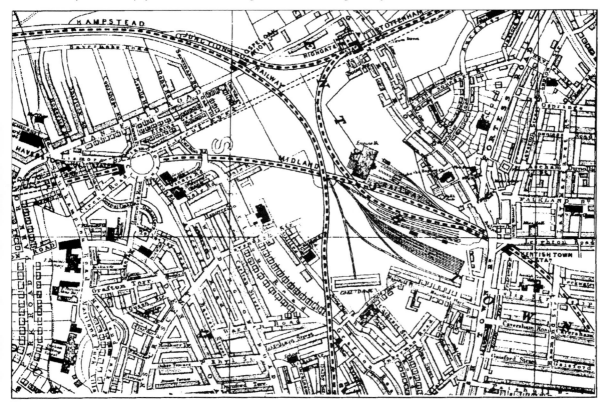

89. *The North London Railway bridge crossing the southern end of Kentish Town Road, by Camden Gardens.*

90. *The bridge of the Tottenham and Hampstead Junction Railway, crossing Highgate Road.*

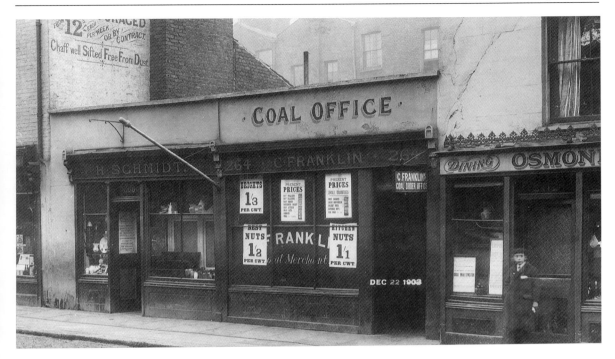

91. Franklin's Coal Office at 264 Kentish Town Road in 1903.

The Midland seized on this site with some vigour, happy to have so many acres for its depots and marshalling yards, reasonably near to their terminus at St Pancras. In buying up land here they took the grounds of Weston's Retreat, west of Kentish Town Road[1], a pleasure ground opened in 1864. This venture, begun by a music-hall owner rather late in the day and out of the way for such entertainments, boasted conservatories with luxuriant flowers, and many gas lights. Unfortunately, the neighbours were able to get a court injunction against him displaying fireworks, balloons and acrobats and playing music. The Retreat was therefore doomed to failure and it closed two years later, just as the Midland needed the land.

After Kentish Town, the Midland line went on to Lismore Circus, where there was a station, and then through tunnels to Finchley Road. The result of all this was that a large area between Highgate Road and Grafton Road was the site of interconnecting railway lines and their necessary buildings A great deal of smoke and noise emanated from this rectangle of old and much excavated farm land, which led to the further reduction of the social status of West Kentish Town and the development of factories on the west side of Highgate Road, such as the large bottling stores just south of Carkers Lane.

London's appetite for coal was vast, and once the Midland had its own London terminus and coal drops north of Holmes Road, it could fully exploit the East Midlands coalfields. At the drops the wagons were emptied from a viaduct into hoppers beneath and then taken away by or to merchants. The depot possessed forty stables for horses, weighing machines and ten offices for merchants. In 1963/4, when British Road Services took over the site, only one merchant was left there.[2]

To add to the passenger traffic, a cross-town facility was added in 1885, when it was possible to come from the Great Eastern Railway at Chingford to Highgate Road - there were twelve trains a day to encourage pleasure trips to Hampstead and the Heath, and three years later the trains went on to Gospel Oak, from which passengers could transfer to a train to Hampstead Heath. This service ran until 1926. Highgate Road station (now occupied by a car repair firm) was opened in 1868 and closed in 1918.

It was at Gospel Oak in 1861, on the North London Line, that one of the more serious early rail accidents took place, with the subsequent lurid illustration in the *Illustrated London News* (ill. 92). A collision occurred between a ballast train and an excursion train travelling from Kew. The engine of the latter crashed over the embankment, dragging with it four or five carriages containing passengers. About 13 or 14 were killed and some sixty hurt. The inquest heard that

92. *A dramatic picture of the railway disaster on the North London Railway in September 1861.*

the accident was caused by a signalman's mistake. He let the passenger train on to the stretch of line without ensuring that it was empty. He was seventeen years old, untrained and really a porter. He was partially deaf, his wages 14 shillings a week and his hours were 15½ one day and ten the next.

Another disaster occurred in 1872 when Kentish Town West station burnt down. Oddly, this station was destroyed by fire in 1972, almost exactly a hundred years afterwards.

THE UNDERGROUND

The Northern line reached Kentish Town in 1907 but observant people will know that another station, between Camden Town and Kentish Town existed near the Castle Inn. South Kentish Town station building still exists and its platforms may be briefly glimpsed on the journey through it. John Betjeman made an engrossing broadcast about it in 1951. "Hardly anyone used the station at all. I should think about three people a day. Every other train on the Underground railway went through without stopping." It was, he said, like a comma in the wrong place of a sentence, and when trains did stop there passengers were annoyed at the delay.

The station was closed in 1924. Betjeman went on to tell the story of one, Basil Green, an income tax inspector who lived in Highgate, who got out at Kentish Town every working day of his life. He knew, even without looking up from his crossword when he had reached Kentish Town, but one Friday, two extraordinary things happened. The train stopped in the tunnel precisely at the platform of the closed and dark South Kentish Town Station, and secondly by some mischance the guard opened the doors. Mr Green, still reading his paper, and without a glance at what he was doing, got out and on to the platform, whereupon the doors closed behind him.

He had no success flagging down trains which followed. He found in the dark the spiral staircase and went up it – all 294 steps, and then bumped his head on the floor of one of the shops which had been built above the staircase since the closure of the station. He banged at the floorboards to no avail. He then found the empty lift shafts and could see a chink of light at the top where another shop was superimposed. Rashly, and bravely, he climbed up the lift shaft, but then, even more carefully he had to climb down again. On the platform still the train drivers took no notice of him and he went to sleep there.

Unfortunately, Betjeman did not finish this Gothic tale. Perhaps there was no ending and he made the whole thing up. Or else the conclusion was too mundane and it spoiled the story.

93. *Fire destroyed Kentish Town West Station in 1872. It is depicted here in the Illustrated London News.*

94. *The old South Kentish Town Underground station. The building still survives.*

A Burst of Churches

HOLY TRINITY

Much of Kentish Town was built from 1845 to 1865 in a frenetic sprint of building by previously cautious estate owners and optimistically speculative builders, sometimes in collusion. Amenities, excepting pubs, were not provided. The area, particularly West Kentish Town, was also seen as being without religion – as indeed it was, since St John's parish church (the old Kentish Town Chapel) in Highgate Road could, even after rebuilding in 1845, seat only 1332 people. It was at this time that St Pancras appointed the Rev. Thomas Dale as its vicar, and it was during his twelve years in office that the whole picture was transformed. A first step in this had already been taken in 1815, when the Chapel became a ministry separate from St Pancras Old Church, and in 1849, a year after Dale's arrival, the parish was divided into sixteen districts. Dale not only had Kentish Town to worry about, but Camden Town and south of the Euston Road as well.

The principle contribution of the Church of England to Kentish Town was the opening of Holy Trinity in Hartland Road in 1850. It was in the very heart of the slum area, but even then out of an accommodation of 1426, only 856 of the seats were free. The church, on land donated by Sir Joseph Hawley and Lewis Buck MP, cost £15,000 to build, of which £5,000 was guaranteed by the first vicar, the energetic Rev. David Laing. Appointed in 1848 and using at first a disused room loaned from a railway company, he persevered in this difficult area to establish a sufficient congregation to warrant a full appeal for a permanent church. He was admired enough to warrant nine pages in an 1874 history of the area[1], but he was obliged to resign in 1857 for he had himself run out of money, and was rewarded with the 'valuable preferment' of St Olave, Hart Street instead.

Holy Trinity, designed by Wyatt and Brandon, was for years the flagship of the Church of England in the area, but it was the Congregationalists who made a great deal of the running. Two of their churches opened within a year of each other – the first in Kelly Street in 1848, and the other, later known as the Haverstock or Gospel Oak Congregational Chapel, in the grounds of the Orphan Working School on Maitland Park Road. The former began at the turn of that century in a room at the east end of Holmes Road and, with the aid of funds from Thomas Wilson of Highbury, the congregation built their own Chapel in Kentish Town Road, opposite Prince of Wales Road (see p.63) in 1807, before the major building in Kelly Street was affordable.

THE METHODISTS

Though the Congregationalists had the greater presence in Kentish Town, the Methodists had begun much earlier.[2] Two of their makeshift chapels are pictured on King's Panorama. One of them is in the unlikely location of Highgate Road, just south of Gordon House Road – its existence today marked by Wesleyan Place. The other is near Fortess Walk. The first appears to have sprung out of regular meetings of farm workers around the Gospel Oak tree located on the boundary of St Pancras and Hampstead. A farm building was offered them (this was a Mortimer family farm) which was later reconstructed as a chapel. The second of the chapels is the earliest. It was built in 1778 by Thomas Walton, on the site of the present fire station in Highgate Road. King mentions it as the "first and only one Established in the village, with no settled Minister, but left open for any itinerant who came gratuitously to do duty, which was usually well attended on every occasion." This building was converted to a private dwelling in 1820 and the chapel replaced by another in Leighton Road, in front of what became a site devoted to social services over the years.

The Wesleyans by the 1860s were doing as well as the Congregationalists. The Leighton Road chapel

95 & 96. Two early Methodist chapels in Kentish Town, depicted by James King on his Panorama. Above, the chapel is in Highgate Road, near Gordon House Road – Wesleyan Place now marks the location. The chapel shown below, for itinerant Methodist preachers, was near today's Fortess Walk.

97. *Holy Trinity in Hartland Road.*

98. The Wesleyan Church in Lady Margaret Road, now used by Roman Catholics.

was superseded in 1864 by a large church in Lady Margaret Road accommodating 1060 people, designed by Edward Tarring. The previous year the congregation which had met in the old farm building in Highgate Road was dislodged by the railway and moved to Bassett Street in West Kentish Town to a small chapel. This was very soon inadequate and instead they built the splendid, Corinthian-pillared building in Prince of Wales Road. In 1904 it was noted that "in Kentish Town and Camden Town the Wesleyans are the strongest body of Nonconformists in every respect, in spiritual vigour, enthusiastic work and self-support. Their church and work in Prince of Wales Road are the best and brightest in all the district; in every department the young people take a growing and active part, and everything throbs with life and goes with a swing. Their ministers have

but to ask, and the thing is done!"

The Wesleyans have fared no better in modern times than most of the other established churches and sects. With increasing costs being borne by a decreasing congregation, the Lady Margaret Road Methodists swapped churches with the Catholics in Fortess Road, and Prince of Wales Road became the Drama Centre stage school.

There were also Primitive Methodists in the area. They had a large chapel in Grafton Road at the corner with Wilkin Street, built in 1867. In recent times its congregation, like that of the Prince of Wales Road church, has joined with the Gospel Oak Methodist Church which itself was formed by a breakaway of members from the Prince of Wales Road building in 1875. In June 1900 they built their own octagonal church at the corner of Lisburne Road – said to be the last building to be made of the red bricks from the Gospel Oak brickworks. This building was replaced by the present church in 1971.

FAST EXPANSION

At a time when it must have seemed that the Christian religion, and the Church of England in particular, had no limits on its expansion, several new large churches were built in Kentish Town. The most striking was St Martin's in Allcroft Road, opened in 1865. Costing £35,000, it was the gift of J. D. Allcroft

99. St. Andrew's, Malden Road, opened in 1866. The architect was Charles Hayward.

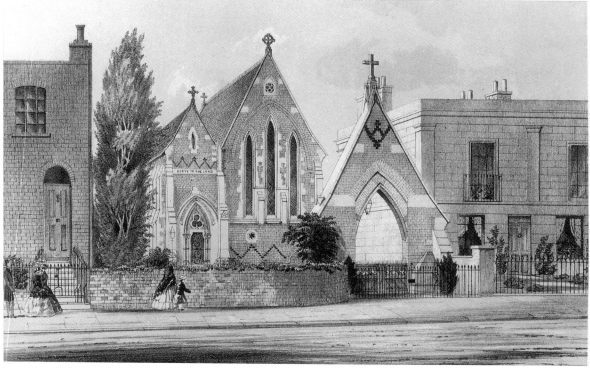

100. *The Free Christian Church in Clarence Road, dedicated in 1855. The minister in charge was a Congregationalist.*

MP of Stokesay Court in Shropshire, a glovemaker by trade, in memory of his wife. He also built the vicarage, mission hall and Sunday schools and gave an endowment. Designed by E.B. Lamb, it is described by Dr Nikolaus Pevsner as "the craziest of London's Victorian churches", and has one of the highest church towers in London.

A year later St Andrew's was opened between 172 and 176 Malden Road. St Luke's was opened in Oseney Crescent in 1869, not only to dignify the Christ Church Estate, but to replace a smaller affair displaced by the Midland Railway at St Pancras. Fine building though it was, it was disliked by a resident of Leighton Road for its high church services and its gas lighting.[3] St Barnabas was opened in Kentish Town Road in 1885 and is now St Andrew's Greek church. What appears to be the last-built parish church is St Silas-the-Martyr, tucked away behind the Prince of Wales Road in Shipton Place. It began as a mission church whose foundation stone was laid by the splendidly named Lady Wilfreda Biddulph in May 1884. It issued its own postcard (ill. 105) depicting its area of activity. The building was replaced by a hotchpotch of a building, designed by E.H. Shearman, in 1912. The following year, it was

in hot water with the Bishop of London who prohibited the performance of a Mystery play there, saying that he thought it undesirable to have a play performed in a church.

Of the later churches, the most important was All Hallows at the corner of Shirlock and Savernake Roads. This area today, with its proximity to Parliament Hill, is now much sought after, but in the 1870s was, as the vicar of nearby St Martin's said, "very similar to an East End parish...The applications to myself for many purposes are almost ceaseless". A mission to help it, both economically and spiritually, was begun in 1878 by Charles Mackeson (hence Mackeson Road), who operated initially from a stable in Fleet Road and then from St Saviour's Mission Hall. So successful was the mission that in 1886 a temporary building, an iron church of the sort used while funds were raised for a gothic replacement, was opened in Mansfield Road. It was called the Church of the Good Shepherd and Mackeson was curate-in-charge. Research by Jane Cox[5] has revealed a level of activity impressive even by the standards of the day. There were fourteen services a week, and between 1886 and 1890 there were 565 baptisms; the average number of communicants in 1890 was 100,

101. St Martin's, Allcroft Road, designed by E.B. Lamb.

with 541 on Easter Day 1889. The Sunday School had ninety teachers and there were numerous societies, including a fife and drum band and a lending library, based on this building.

Soon, this could no longer be contained in a temporary iron building seating 850. Mackeson set about raising the money for a new church with his customary energy, but he had the good fortune to receive £20,000 from the sale of the site of All Hallows in Upper Thames Street, which had been demolished. As Jane Cox notes, the creation of a new parish for All Hallows caused much grief to the vicar of St Martin's, who lost his relatively better-off areas in the rearrangement. The laying of the foundation stone was performed in 1892 by the Duchess of Teck, who came by train to Gospel Oak and then by open carriage along a flag-bedecked Mansfield Road. It was a premature celebration, for there were delays

102. St Luke's, Oseney Crescent.

103. The Mothers' Union attached to St Luke's, Oseney Crescent, between the wars.

Terrace. His company was innovative, including amongst its activities the manufacture of artificial limbs – some of its products may be seen in the collection of the Wellcome Institute, now housed at the Science Museum.[4] When in 1874 Grove End House, Grove End Villa and Grove End Lodge, three houses at the southern end of Grove Terrace, came on the market, Coxeter bought two of them. He presented Grove End Villa to the London Baptist Association which had as its aim the opening of at least one Baptist chapel each year in the metropolis or suburbs. The Villa was pulled down, a building fund established and the church opened in 1877, the work of the cousins, G.F. Satchell and H.O. Edwards.

Kentish Town's first Catholic church, St Alexis, was a private foundation in 1849. It was in Highgate Road, just opposite today's Carrol Place, and was the work of the Rev. Hardinge Ivers who, according to newspaper cuttings in the Heal Collection, "died for want of proper medical aid and nourishment" in College Lane in 1868. According to the same cuttings, he was a descendant of the old Kentish Town land-owners, the Ive family (see p. 25). After forming the church he quarrelled with Cardinal Wiseman, and following a law suit he was expelled the church and lost so much of his property that he became destitute.

The Rev. Ivers' chapel was eventually replaced by a Roman Catholic church in Fortess Road which, as we have seen above, was exchanged with the Wesleyans in Lady Margaret Road in the 1970s. In Southampton Road, St Dominic's Priory was built in 1869, followed by the very large parochial church designed by Charles Alban Buckler in 1883.

Numerous mission halls were to be found in West Kentish Town. Some were of substance, such as Lyndhurst Hall in Warden Road, built by the Lyndhurst Road Congregational church in Hampstead at the turn of this century. Some of them were merely spaces beneath railway arches. All of them have gone except the Hope Chapel in Prince of Wales Road, which began in Hatton Garden in 1837, and after several moves prevailed upon Mr Weeding (from whom Weedington Road is named) to sell them a site on favourable terms. In 1870 its members were described 'simply as Christians'. Their rigorous posters still draw the attention of passers-by.

Not much is known about the North-West London Synagogue in Caversham Road, which was consecrated in October 1900.

in raising the rest of the money needed and Mackeson died in 1899. The Church of All Hallows, still unfinished, was consecrated in 1901, though only a gift from Lord Mansfield provided a roof so that the nave could be consecrated seven years later. The architect of the church was Henry Brook, though the chancel was added by Giles Gilbert Scott in 1908-14.

The main Baptist presence was the Highgate Road Chapel. This was formed by James Coxeter, surgical instrument maker of Grafton Way, who lived at a house called Bathurst in The Grove, opposite Grove

104. *'Temporary Roman Catholic Church of St Mary, adjoining the old manor house, Kentish Town, 1857.' This church presumably superseded the Rev. Ivers' church in Highgate Road, but its location is unknown. It may have been on the site eventually used for St Mary's R.C. church (now occupied by the Methodists).*

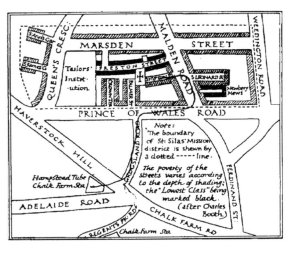

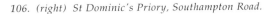

105. *(above) A postcard issued by the St Silas Mission, Shipton Place, indicating the area of West Kentish Town in which it would be working.*

106. *(right) St Dominic's Priory, Southampton Road.*

107. *A desolate street in West Kentish Town, thought to be Litcham Street. It was demolished by the St Pancras House Improvement Society and replaced by Athlone Street.*

Slums and Saviours

In Charles Booth's poverty map of London (1889) he painted his darker colours in West Kentish Town. His enquiries began in 1886 and he and his researchers painstakingly surveyed each street in central London (Kentish Town station marks the northern extremity) assessing the occupations and incomes of residents. He found that about 30 per cent of Londoners were in poverty and the rest in comfort. The East End and docklands were, inevitably, areas singled out as the poorest, but north of the Thames West Kentish Town must have given rise to some concern. While we find Malden Road and Queens Crescent as either comfortable or fairly so, we find the Weedington Road area classified as poor, with Litcham Street (now Athlone Street) as very poor. The area now covered by the Talacre Open Space and Interchange Studio is mixed poor and comfortable, between St Leonard's Square and Prince of Wales Road is very poor as is one of the streets across Malden Road. South of Prince of Wales Road it is a similar story on both sides of Ferdinand Street. In the area of Kentish Town covered by the survey, only Caversham Road, Oseney Crescent, the Bartholomew Estate roads, Maitland Park Road and the southern end of Willes Road warrant Mr Booth's classification of well-to-do.

The awfulness of Litcham Street was even worse when visited by workers for the St Pancras House Improvement Society, when it was registered in 1924. In one house there a family of thirteen lived on the ground floor of a house so darkened by the buildings at the rear that light came only from the street side. In a booklet published by the Society in 1931 there is a description of a house of 12 rooms which housed eight families, and it was reported that in many houses "male members of families had to turn out into the streets for a short time in order that their sisters might retire for the night in a little comfort, and that they in their turn had to undress in the dark." In 1937 it was announced that many local people spent only three shillings a week on food. The Society's flats in Litcham Street were opened in 1933, and the street renamed Athlone Street. The Society was rewarded for its enterprise by an invitation from the LMS railway to develop an open site at the southern end of York Rise to rehouse people that the LMS was displacing for an enlargement of Euston Station. The five blocks, containing 120 flats, were opened in 1938. Many of the tenants then were railway workers whose families had settled around the terminus.

The Society (now the St Pancras Housing Association) still has a strong presence in Kentish Town and

108. Leonard Day House and Priestley House on the Athlone Street Estate.

St Pancras, particularly in Somers Town where much of its earlier work took place.

St Pancras Borough Council began building houses in earnest in the 1930s. Kennistoun House in Leighton Road was finished in 1934 and plans were announced for new flats in Ferdinand and Harmood Streets and Powlett Place. Denyer House on the Highgate Road was built at the same time as the Improvement Society was building the York Rise estate next door, and just as war broke out Montague Tibbles House (now Penshurst) was completed in Prince of Wales Road (Tibbles was a former borough councillor). In this building St Pancras completed its 1000th flat. Other pre-war developments included the Becontree-like houses and flats around the top of Croftdown Road, Kenbrook House in Leighton Road and Una House in Prince of Wales Road.

In 1955 the Council opened its 2,000th post-war flat, but even then the housing programme was still in an early stage. By the end of the 1960s the Council, then the London Borough of Camden, had rebuilt half of Castlehaven Road, parts of Ferdinand Street and Carltoun Street (off Warden Road) and had bought up much of the Christ Church Estate. In the

109. Opening of the Athlone Street housing in 1933. To the right are the Mayor of St Pancras, the Princess Alice, and Stanley Shaw of St Pancras House Improvement Society..

following fifteen years it demolished, redrew and replaced much of the rest of West Kentish Town, particularly around Lismore Circus and on both sidea of Prince of Wales Road. It also developed the previously unused land, called 'The Alps' by local children, behind College Lane.

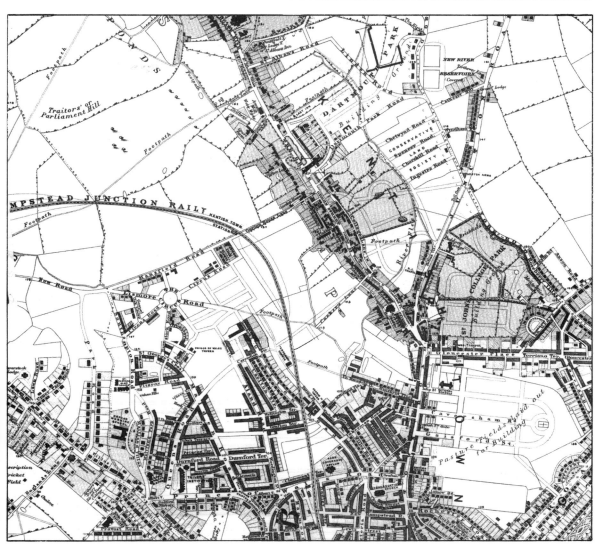

110. *Stanford's map of 1862 shows a built-up Kentish Town in the south, and poised for development of the estates in the north. Note the ominous words 'Building Ground' on the St John's College Estate.*

Body and Mind

THE SOCIAL VILLAGERS

There is in Camden's Local History Collection a pamphlet published in 1822 by Septimus Miles. *The Senate; or Social Villagers of Kentish Town* is in the form of a *canto*, and describes the regular assemblies of the elite of Kentish Town. It is difficult to assess if the mainly jocular tone has a malicious purpose. At times it is barbed, at times without harm. The assemblies met, of course, "At Englefield's", who managed the Assembly House, where their deliberations became more profound as the evenings wore on:

"At Englefield's, in form, these Statesmen meet
To crown a victor or condemn defeat;
Nectareous draughts soon make the vista clear
And space condensing brings all objects near."

Members of this group included neighbours of the author, such as 'sententious' Latchford. Dealt with at length is Thomas King, the father of the artist James King.

"Lo! in his chair, with magisterial ease
Fam'd for his memory, famous for green peas
Sits Thomas King, the king's right faithful squire
Whose cot and garden modestly retire,
Where shelt'ring Elms the gothic castle screen."

Also mentioned is William Agar, who lived in Elm Lodge off St Pancras Way and Andrew Mensal, headmaster of Gordon House Academy, described as

"... classic Mensal, liberally kind
By nature form'd to mould the ductile mind."

The assembly as a whole Miles portrays as:

"Builders of churches, menders of highways
Who bought the organ that great Wesley plays
Enlarg'd the Chapel, made brave Wiber [a builder] rich..."

Miles is describing here a Kentish Town that would soon disappear together with the influence that these well-heeled drinking companions had in the parish. Forty years on, as the map in illustration 110 demonstrates, the old Kentish Town was almost gone for ever, as the estates were prepared for development. In 1822, when the 'Social Villagers' were quaffing at the Assembly House, the Vestry power base was set to move southwards mainly to the burgeoning area south of the Euston Road, leaving Kentish Town, in comparison, a rather old-fashioned village. These men gathered at the Assembly House were most probably long dead by the time that Kentish Town

itself expanded with a crushing rapidity. Their comfortable world was bothered and then dislodged by the problems caused by a massive growth of slums, poverty and bad hygiene. The resources of the parish they had run could barely tackle, let alone solve them. Even the reform of metropolitan government in 1855 failed to compel local authorities like St Pancras to raise enough money to deal with a worsening situation. Instead, ratepayers (the poor did not pay rates) dug their heels in and almost invariably gave ground when too late or when ordered to.

But St Pancras Vestry was not just slow in responding to the situation, but *notoriously* slow. Successive medical officers of health despaired at the attitude of their elected masters. In 1875, Dr Stevenson, the then Medical Officer of Health, resigned because the Vestry declined to allow him the staff to inspect sanitary conditions. In the same year the Vestry refused to co-operate in the compulsory notification of contagious diseases. Stevenson's resignation was not accepted and eventually a compromise was worked out, though it is interesting to note that at that time he was by no means a full-time employee of the Vestry. After accepting the withdrawal of his resignation the Vestry demanded that he spent at least three hours a day at the Vestry offices. The problem for Stevenson was that the Vestry simply did not pay enough to its Medical Officer and he had to do private work to make ends meet. Yet in reality, St Pancras needed not just a full-time medical officer, but an amplitude of sanitary staff as well.

Stevenson's successor, Mr Shirley Murphy, fared no better. In 1885 he too resigned complaining that "the protracted enquiry now pending has shown me that the most exceptional and unscrupulous means are being adopted to discredit me for the sake of preventing effectual sanitary work." His job, he said, was "of no avail against interests opposed to sanitary reform."

BATHS PROVIDED

There is no doubt that the Vestry was careful in its expenditure on sanitary mprovements, although they and their successors, St Pancras Council (1899) were enthusiastic about baths and washhouses. Even those vestrymen most reluctant to spend ratepayers' money, and who thought that the poor generally deserved their poverty, agreed that it was in the public interest that they should be clean. Baths for swimming and bathing, and washhouses for laundry, were regarded as legitimate expenditure.

The first public baths in the parish opened in Plender Street, Camden Town in 1868. Nearly a year later the Vestry reported that it had been used by over 145,000 people, though at first the laundry facilities were under-used. It was noted that a large number

111. *The Prince of Wales Road Baths, soon after their opening in 1901. They were designed by Thomas Aldwinckle.*

112. *An interior scene in the new Baths.*

113. *The site of the Prince of Wales Road Baths. A grimy Grafton Road leads into the distance.*

114. *Inside the Baths, 1901.*

of women who did use the laundry were of humble circumstances – the average time taken for washing drying, ironing and mangling the family linen was 3½ hours at a cost of 5½d. Almost certainly these women were doing some other family's washing as well as their own.

Encouraged by the success of Plender Street, the Vestry opened a second baths in Whitfield Street, near Tottenham Court Road, in 1879. But it was some time before Kentish Town, very much in need of such an establishment, was provided. The site chosen in Kentish Town was already covered with rather grim houses (see ill. 113). Given the usual meanness of St Pancras, the Prince of Wales Road Baths could easily have been a building without distinction. Fortunately, it was built in one of the golden eras of architecture (1901), when terra cotta was liberally used. But the Baths also represented the first public building erected by the new borough council and no doubt there was a touch of keeping ahead of the neighbours in the lavish specifications for these baths.

It contained four swimming pools – two each for men and women, first and second class – and 129 'slipper' baths (shallow baths in separate cubicles). The laundry had fifty washing cubicles, fifty heated drying horses and a mangling and drying room. Illustration 115 suggests that there was either a separate provision for men, or a special time for them to do their laundry.

The building, designed by Thomas Aldwinckle with terra cotta tiles supplied by Doulton, was opened on 9 October 1901 by Sir Blundell Maple, whose furniture firm had made him wealthy enough to fund the building of University College Hospital.

NO TO BOOKS

The Vestry's attitude towards the provision of public libraries was entirely different. It was hostile to the adoption of the Public Libraries Act, and its opposition was confirmed by the borough council for much of the first half of the twentieth century. St Pancras became notorious in this respect as well.

The earliest public library in Kentish Town was a short-lived one. Some local residents in 1859 announced a meeting to establish a free public reading room and library. They obtained permission to use the old Paving Commissioners' premises in Junction Road and, despite the presence of the parish fire engine there, the library opened. However, in 1863 the organisation dissolved, with no reason stated in the Vestry minutes. In 1882 the Camden Town and Kentish Town Working Men's Club held a concert in aid of a library but no more is known of this.

St Pancras Council, when it was formed in 1899, inherited no library at all. At ratepayers' polls in 1894 and 1898 a majority of those who voted opposed the

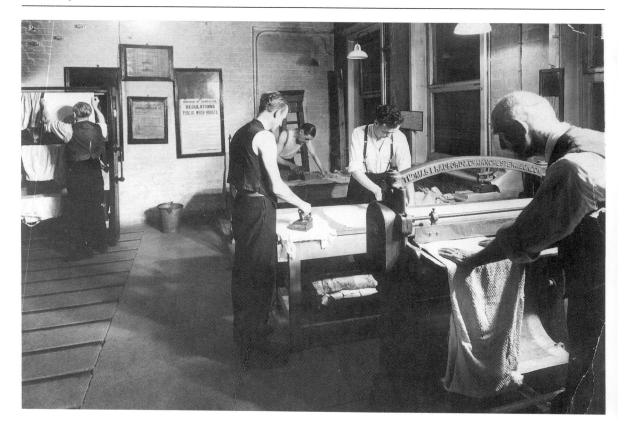

115. *Men doing their laundry at the Prince of Wales Road Baths in 1901.*

116. *A gymnastic display at the Baths.*

adoption of the Public Libraries Act. But politically, things had changed since the rise of the Progressives – a mix of Liberals, Socialists and Fabians – in local politics. The enthusiasm which had swept them to power when the London County Council had been formed ten years earlier had still not dissipated, and in St Pancras they took control of the first borough council. Eager to seem progressive they encouraged the campaign to establish libraries, anxious to claim the largesse being offered to local councils by the philanthropist Andrew Carnegie. Many ratepayers and their spokesmen on the Council were still opposed however. The Camden Town estate agent, Westmacott, said in one of the debates that "Books of reference can be seen free at the British Museum by all who care to take the trouble", and implied that those who read works of fiction should not be encouraged to do so by the borough council.

Islington in 1904 adopted the Act on the understanding that Carnegie would provide £40,000 to-

117. (above) The public library in a converted shop/house in
Malden Road.

118. (right) The East Kentish Town public library in a
converted house in Fortess Road.

wards the cost of various library buildings. And when in 1905 Carnegie offered a similar arrangement to St Pancras they accepted on the basis that they would spend up to 1d in the £1 rate on a central library and four branches on sites which were to be free of the 1d rate.

Unfortunately, St Pancras found it difficult to obtain free sites from other philanthropic people. The only one it gathered was the virtually inaccessible piece of land in Chester Road in what was called Highgate New Town, for which the Duke of Bedford put up the required £500.   In the circumstances Carnegie agreed to allow the borough to *purchase* a site for the central library, and deduct the loan interest charges from the 1d rate. The site chosen and its price caused quite a stir among sceptical ratepayers. Like the baths it was in Prince of Wales Road, between Willes Road and Grafton Yard – the Council flats, Una House, now stand there. The problem for opponents was that the site cost over £15,000 and was owned by a Progressive St Pancras alderman, Horace Regnart. Despite the protracted negotiations, the borough went ahead and appointed a Chief Librarian, Henry Bond, at £350 per annum.

The library at Chester Road was officially opened on 18 October 1906. Enthusiasm for libraries was so high that the borough proposed a whole system of buildings which would be open to the public every day except Sundays and holidays from 10am to 9.30pm. The enthusiasm was short lived, for at the next local elections the Progressives were voted out, and the Municipal Reformers – a mix of Conservatives and ratepayers' association members – were voted in. One of their first actions was to cancel work on the central library where the site had already been cleared.

A rowdy meeting at the Town Hall in November 1907 rallied to the support of public libraries. Furthermore, the Council found that it might not be legal for them to dispose of the site because it had been bought as part and parcel of an agreement with Carnegie using a levied 1d rate to pay the interest charges. In 1908 the poor chief librarian was given notice, since there was no library system in the offing, though they kept him on for some time on a humiliating six-month contract at half salary. The Municipal Reformers did not wish to seek a ruling by the Local Government Board about the disposal of the site in case the LGB said that it was illegal: then St Pancras would *have* to build a library in Prince of

119. *The North Western Polytechnic in its final and briefest guise as part of the University of North London.*

Wales Road. Carnegie, for his part, cannily did not withdraw his offer, thereby locking St Pancras into the bargain they had struck in earlier and happier days.

Years later the Council did decide to invite the LGB to consider the matter. A public enquiry was held in front of a sympathetic Inspector who expressed the opinion during the proceedings that "public libraries were discredited owing to their large issue of fiction". He declined to hear evidence of the success of libraries in other boroughs.

In 1914 the LGB made its decision – the Council could sell the site, and in August the much chastened Chief Librarian found a job at Portsmouth where, bowed down by lack of money and allegations of theft, he committed suicide.

The attitude of St Pancras Council towards libraries did not improve between the wars, though the mayor of the borough, when launching a mobile library during the Second World War, had the temerity to proclaim that "Books will strengthen us to beat Hitler". No more libraries were built until the later years of the borough's existence in the 1960s, though a branch library opened in a converted house in Camden Street in 1921. In Kentish Town the same solution was used for many years. In 1949 an East Kentish Town branch was begun in a house at 104 Fortess Road, which remained in use until the purpose-built library next to the Underground station was opened in 1962. In West Kentish Town the Council used a house in Malden Road from 19 October 1946; this branch transferred to a building in Athlone Street in 1967 and then to a new library opened in Queens Crescent in 1978.

EDUCATING THE EDUCATED

It was fortunate that the provision of education was not at that time the responsibility of local authorities. We may be sure that in St Pancras the Board Schools would have been built to a much lower standard and that little provision for further education would have been made. In the 1920s enthusiasm for the Polytechnic movement, begun by Quintin Hogg and fostered by such organisations as the Working Men's College, was still strong. On a fairly empty site in Prince of Wales Road (facing what would have been the Central Library if it had been built) the North-Western Polytechnic was opened by the Prince of Wales in October 1929. Its history was conventional until the disturbed years of the early 1970s when militant students demonstrated regularly against the Director of the Polytechnic, Terence Miller. The Polytechnic was absorbed into the Polytechnic of

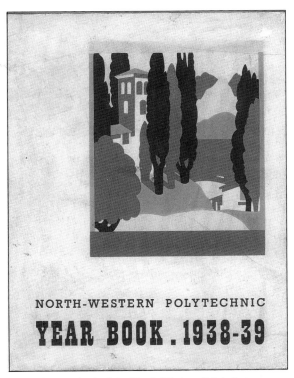

120. *The year-book of the North-Western Polytechnic, 1938-39.*

North London in Islington and as that rebuilt itself along the Holloway Road, the future of Kentish Town's building seemed more and more in doubt. The Polytechnic became the University of North London, but in 1996 it was closed down in Kentish Town, leaving an already neglected building empty. It is now being converted into apartments and hopefully this building, designed by W.E. Riley, will be renovated to a condition where its architectural merits may be properly assessed.

Not far from the Polytechnic is the well-known Evening Institute at Holmes Road. In the 1920s the LCC closed the building as an elementary school because of a falling population, and from then on it was synonymous with adult education. A Junior Men's Institute was set up in 1927 for boys judged to be "least capable of profiting by academic courses". They were encouraged to plan their own vocational courses, which included practical skills and sports, though there was some music as well. The Kentish Town Camera Club met here from 1924, as did the Kentish Town Weightlifting Club.

Trading Places

Shops are the best barometer of social change. Their size, specialities, location and profitability are the most accurate indications of a community's ups and downs. Kentish Town's heyday as a shopping centre was between the wars when most of the chain stores of the day were present, but combined with a strong presence of independent traders. Locals might be tempted to go up to Holloway for the more sophisticated delights of the Jones Brothers store, or to the cheaper prices of Queens Crescent market, but generally the shops in Kentish Town Road were the complete providers.

C & A DANIELS

The principal shop was C & A Daniels, drapers who had expanded shop by shop as was customary in most Victorian high streets until they had a sufficient concentration of units to warrant rebuilding as a single store. This the Daniels brothers began to do

after they bought the freehold of some of their shops, on the site of the medieval Kentish Town Chapel, in 1926. What they did rebuild may still be seen behind modern shop fronts at nos 217-223 Kentish Town Road. The business began with one shop, called The Little Wonder in 1865.[1] It was the drapers who made the money in Victorian days. The cheap availability of seamstresses and servants to make and look after the excessive furnishings and voluminous clothing which had become fashionable, coupled with a growing prosperity and middle class, made these shops into emporiums where the mistress of the house, and not the servants, did the ordering. There was too an enormous demand for mourning clothes, so much so that even Daniels had its own shop for these.

Many of the shop assistants lived on the premises and the hours were long. V.S. Pritchett in his book *A Cab at the Door*, recalls that his parents met at the store where his father worked as a shopwalker, and his mother as a milliner. "She was so quick with the customers...and so clever with trimmings! She could put an ugly hat on a grumbling woman, give a twist, snatch a feather or a bunch of cherries and so dazzle the customer with chatter and her smiles." The hours

121. *Some of the original shops of C & A Daniels in Kentish Town Road, 1903.*

were 8 to 8 on weekdays, and until 11 on Saturday nights. No wonder that the staff, who ate in the basement and slept in the attics, went out, as Pritchett noted, and got drunk when the shop closed for the day. Pritchett's mother admitted to quite a few pranks during her employment there, including putting fly-papers on old Daniels' chair.

But Daniels', like so many of the drapers which became miniature department stores, did not survive modern competition. Drapery became a diminished field, cheap clothing could be had at Marks & Spencer, Dunn's and Burton's, Woolworth's sold household goods, as did Timothy White's, and residents of Kentish Town had the Underground to take them to the larger choice offered by Oxford Street. Nevertheless, the shop celebrated its 87th birthday in 1952. Then, as Gillian Tindall noted[2], "The Beverley Sisters signed their latest record in the newly-opened television department and prizes were offered in a knitting competition. One lifelong customer brought in a packet of needles which her mother had pur-

chased at the store in 1870, and every hundredth customer was offered a free permanent wave."

The Daniels' shop was not the only large drapers in the road. At nos 293-299 (on the north corner of Holmes Road) and also at 303-305 was Herbert Beddall, who rebuilt his row of shops as a single store in 1900 (see ill. 122).

DUNN'S THE HATTERS

A nationally known Kentish Town business was Dunn's, the clothiers and hatters, which made its reputation at a time when almost every man wore a hat or cap of some kind. By 1895 George Arthur Dunn had established a warehouse at the top of Royal College Street, which also fronted Kentish Town Road on its west side – the site, indeed, of our front jacket illustration. These premises were, in effect, a central depot from which orders were distributed to well over 100 branches. Charles Nisbitt, who worked there from 1930 until 1979, rose to become the chief

122. *Herbert Beddall's drapery stores, 293-299 Kentish Town Road, on the corner with Holmes Road.*

buyer of headgear. He remembers Dunn as a stickler for timekeeping, whose presence was almost invariably accompanied by a large cigar. Dunn's in Kentish Town closed down in 1984 and after some changes of ownership which failed to re-establish the name among clothes buyers, the company ceased trading within the past year.

AT QUEENS CRESCENT

The most famous retailing name in the area – at least in the future – was John Sainsbury. He and his wife (she the daughter of a dairyman in Chalton Street, Somers Town) opened their first shop selling milk, eggs, cheese and butter in Drury Lane in 1869. It was one of hundreds of similar businesses in London – there were five such in Drury Lane alone – but the Sainsburys, despite an ever increasing family, were unusually hard workers and good business people. In 1876 they opened a branch at 159 Queens Crescent, and moved their home there as well. Another branch was opened a few doors away in 1878, which traded until 1968. Their first employee, William Goodwin, was taken on at this shop, where they also had a stall outside in the market.

"He used to get up early and wait behind the shop door with trestles and boards to set up the stall on the street when the whistle blew to open the market. Getting a pitch needed speed and muscle. Goodwin always made it to the kerbside against any competition. He was a tough man who became resident

124. *John Sainsbury and his wife in 1896, founders of the Sainsbury chain of food stores.*

123. *Queens Crescent market, c.1905.*

125. *Interior of Sainsbury's shop at 159 Queens Crescent in 1950.*

126. *The Sainsbury offices, warehouses and bacon stoves in Allcroft Road, probably in the late 1870s.*

J. SAINSBURY, Provision Merchant,

Office & Warehouses, ALLCROFT ROAD, KENTISH TOWN.

Branch Establishments:—159, 151 & 94, QUEEN'S CRESCENT, HAVERSTOCK HILL;
173, DRURY LANE, HOLBORN; and 68, WATNEY STREET, COMMERCIAL ROAD, E.

J. SAINSBURY has now removed his Wholesale Business from 173, Drury Lane, to more extensive premises situate in Allcroft Road, Kentish Town, and has made the necessary alterations to carry on a larger retail trade at the above address; he therefore begs his customers to understand that the same quality goods are sold as those so much admired by his wholesale customers, and as he is a large Importer of all kinds of provisions, is enabled to offer them at first cost.

One trial will give universal satisfaction.

Note the Address—173, DRURY LANE.   Note the Address—173, DRURY LANE.

127. *Rayner's, pork butchers at 74, Queens Crescent, c.1926.*

foreman of the Bacon Stoves and Stables when the firm moved to Blackfriars."[3]

This memory of William Goodwin grabbing a market stall in 1876 suggests that the market had been in Queens Crescent virtually since it was built, because that part of the street was not much older.

It was a hard part of London. An old resident, Alfred Grosch, remembered that in about 1900 "people were brutal and pugnacious" and that "when money went on drink others suffered, usually children. Barefoot, hungry children, clad in rags were a common sight as they racked over the refuse heaps of Queens Crescent in search of half rotten fruit."

Mrs Carter, an old stall holder recalled that fresh produce was brought from Covent Garden market, which meant that her husband rose at 4am each working day, taking a horse and cart to collect supplies. The market traded until 10.30pm on Fridays and after midnight on Saturdays. Between the wars inhabitants from the new northern suburbs, such as Hendon, used to travel to Queens Crescent on Saturday nights by train from Colindale to Lismore Circus, as their own shops had shut for the day.

Sainsbury opened bacon stoves and stabling in Allcroft Road (see ill. 126). This was not, it seems, an unusual location for such a business. Desmond

Whyman has done some interesting research on the butchers' shops of Kentish Town[4] and found that West Kentish Town was a centre of the butchery trade and for slaughterhouses. The nearness of the railway cattle depots to the east, and the generally run-down nature of the area would have encouraged what many people thought of as a noxious trade. In the Vestry minutes in July 1856, it was noted that slaughtering (in the parish of St Pancras) was carried on by each butcher however and whenever he wishes without regard to the neighbourhood, often densely populated. There is usually little drainage and solid animal matter can go into the sewer."

When in 1856 the Vestry first issued licences for slaughterhouses, there were about 115 in St Pancras parish, which included many in West Kentish Town. As Mr Whyman points out, the old established butchers in Kentish Town Road were used to doing their own slaughtering and for that purpose needed either a side or rear entrance to the premises so that animals could be brought there. These butchers were therefore to be found generally in those premises on either side of Kentish Town Road which had a mews at the rear.

The Holmes family itself owned a slaughterhouse behind the west side of Kentish Town Road, and went even further by having a tannery to cure the hides. The aptly named Giles Silverside rented land from the Christ Church Estate so as to rear cattle for market. One prominent butcher at 317 Kentish Town Road from *c*.1907 until 1955, was George Kimber. After George V recovered from illness in 1928 aided by newly-invented electro-therapuetic treatment, Kimber astonished members of the St Pancras Rotary Club by specially attending a Rotary council meeting to offer them £10,000 to provide a sun-ray unit for local residents. This became the Camden Town Clinic.[5]

INDEPENDENT TRADERS

Typical of the smaller traders in the main road was the bookshop and stationer's of Bishop & Hamilton. Frank Bishop began it *c*.1894, and took on a young lad without formal education called Hamilton. The boy was able in 1914 to buy the firm, though Bishop remained, spending much time in the basement 'writing' mysteriously. Most of the trade then was

in books, particularly a Twopenny Library. Mr Hamilton's son joined the firm when he was fourteen and served there until he retired in 1979. His reminiscences on retirement[6] included a corn-chandler across the road, and a next door neighbour, a greengrocer, who did a trade in horses on the side, using a piece of land at the rear rented from the Midland Railway.

Other long-term traders who are remembered by many people today, include W. Flint in Fortess Road, whose delightful old shop sold tools, nuts and bolts, ironmongery etc. This business is shown in the 1892 street directory as a brass finisher. Thos. H. Smerdon (never Thomas!), just north of the Assembly House, began as an electrical engineer *c*.1911 at the corner of Fortess Road and Falkland Road, but prominent in the area before that was Robert Smerdon, builder and decorator who, it has been said, built the western end of Croftdown Road. The timber merchant George Bignell Elliott had, by the 1890s, premises in Fortess Road, Gillies Street and Queens Crescent; Buttles in Castle Road, also timber suppliers, claim to have been

128. *Bishop & Hamilton's shop in Kentish Town Road, before Hamilton added his name.*

in business since 1919. For longevity, as in most parts
of London, few traders can match the undertakers.
In 1922 Kentish Town Road had Frederick Richards
at the corner with Castle Road, William Beckett in
Junction Road and Alfred Madley in Malden Road.
All these names are familiar in those streets today.

By 1932 Kentish Town Road included many of the
chain stores of the day – all on the west side. At 247
there was Boot's, at 253 Home & Colonial, 257 Lipton's,
293 Burton's, 299 Lyon's teashop, 303 Marks &
Spencer, 313 Dewhurst's, 329 Woolworth's, 343
Dunn's and at 345 Jay's furniture. Some minor chains
were on the east side, including Sainsbury at 194, the
ABC bakery at 202, Walton Hassell & Port at 204, and
the London Co-op at 122.

129. *W.H. Walkley, bakers, at 265 Kentish Town Road in
1903.*

130. *Henry Merralls and Son, master farriers, of 63 Fc
Road, c.1906.*

131. *Alf Matthews, milkman in Kentish Town and Gospel Oak during the 1920s. His brother, Bert, was the Pearly King for Hampstead.*

132. *William Doughty, builder and decorator at 107 Kentish Town Road in 1903. Note the plaque inscribed 'Providence Place, 1810', the old name for the terrace.*

133. *Edwin Cossor, bookbinder, at 103 Castle Road, early nineteenth century.*

134. *Park's Dairy in Kentish Town Road. Behind is the surviving part of the Vicarage once attached to Kentish Town Chapel.*

135. *The offices of Salter Rex, the most prominent estate agents in Kentish Town at the time, at 311 Kentish Town Road.*

136. *(above) The second-hand shop of H.S. Judge of Lismore Circus.*

137. *(below) A.E. Lacy, plumber, at 177 Kentish Town Road in 1903.*

138. *(right) An advertisement for tobacconists H. Kalb, 184 Kentish Town Road, in 1907.*

WISDOM

3 POINTS FOR AN INTELLIGENT PIPE-SMOKER TO REMEMBER

WHY YOU SHOULD NOT SMOKE WET TOBACCO

1. It is not healthy! It does not produce the **beneficial effects** that pipe-smoking is intended to give.

2. It makes your pipes foul and inconveniences your associates especially your **feminine ones.**

3. It is not economical as the 32% of moisture allowed in tobacco **deprives you** of nearly one-third the nett weight tobacco. It means you get a little over $\frac{2}{3}$ of an oz. instead of 1 oz.

HOW MUCH WOULD YOU GIVE TO PREVENT YOUR PIPE FROM BEING FOUL?

I introduce a tobacco which does away with all these evils. It is in 3 strengths.

Sun-dried Virginia · Very mild.
Havana Cut Claro · Medium.
Havana Cut Madura · Full.

Per 1/0½ oz.
You can blend them
to your liking.

WHILE SMOKING IT. *(It's Pleasure.)*

AFTER SMOKING IT *(It's Economy.)*

H. KALB.
184, Kentish Town Road, N.W.

Phone : **6127** Hamp.

139. *Robbery in Kentish Town, 1886. This sub-post office, which was also a chemist, stood at the junction of Brecknock and Lady Margaret Roads. George Finch entered the shop one afternoon, demanded the cashbox and on being refused, shot the assistant through the head. He managed to escape with the box back to his house, 15 Ospringe Road, where he was traced. He was nineteen and said to be an art student..*

The Social Side

SOCIETIES

Kentish Town has had few social societies. There was in the nineteenth century a Kentish Town Music Appreciation Society which paid for the installation of a monument to the composer, Charles Dibdin, in the burial ground of St Martin-in-the-Fields off Camden Street. The Kentish Town Literary Society was established in 1849 with the aim of stimulating interesting literature. It was successful for a time – when it held its Annual Meeting in 1852 in rooms opposite Prince of Wales Road, over 400 people attended. It was announced then that a gentleman called Dendy had offered £700 for ground on the site of the old Assembly House (presumably in Leighton Road), on which he proposed to build, at a cost of some thousands a magnificent literary institution and theatre for the use of Kentish Town inhabitants. This got no further than the attempts to build a Central Library in Prince of Wales Road.

A humanist with the unlikely name of Stanton Coit established what he called a 'Neighbourhood Guild' in Kentish Town in 1889. An American, Coit had already formed such organisations in New York, building on the enthusiasm of neighbours to form themselves into social clubs. In Kentish Town he lived at 7 Leighton Crescent and it was in his house that the Kentish Town Neighbourhood Guild began with a full programme of lectures, dances and other activities. However, they appear to have also been using a 24-room mansion called Leighton Hall for such activities. The only property which would begin to match this specification is Montpelier House off Brecknock Road, the garden of which backed on to Coit's own premises.

The 1895 report of the Guild detailed choral and orchestral societies, lecture courses etc, and a social life of garden parties and dances. In 1902 Leighton Hall 'was disposed of'.

Very few sporting clubs have survived for long. We know of a cricket game featuring gentlemen from Kentish Town and Hampstead as early as 1794, when some very extravagant wagers were placed on the result. The nearest that Kentish Town has had to a general sporting club has been the Mansfield Bowling Club, to be found on the site of Parliament Hill School for Girls in 1907, and by 1911, presumably displaced by school building, at its present base at Croftdown Road. In Talacre Road the St Pancras Amateur Boxing Club, established in 1900, has its premises.

140. A cricket match in 1794, on Highgate Common, between eleven gentlemen of Highgate, and eleven gentlemen of Kentish Town and Hampstead. The wager on the result was four hundred guineas.

CINEMAS

Until recent times, when plays were presented at the Bull & Gate, Kentish Town has had no theatre. It has now no cinemas either, but two of the old picture houses survive.[1]

The earliest cinema in Kentish Town was in Malden Road. The Gem Picture House, which opened in 1910, seated only about 460. It had several changes of name, finishing as The Court, a name used by a petrol station which in recent years occupied its site.

In the same year as The Gem, the Kentish Town Cinema, or The Gaisford, opened at the corner of Gaisford Street and Kentish Town Road. It too was a small building, seating about 500, and its stage was only six feet deep. Surprisingly, this tiny picture house continued in business until 1960, when it was demolished and replaced by apartments called Northumberland House.

An open-air cinema was begun in Prince of Wales Road in 1911 run by Ernest Mansell, who had earlier presented moving pictures at Kentish Town Baths opposite. The site consisted of the gardens of the local Reform Club, and was subsequently that of the North-Western Polytechnic. The Garden Cinema, of necessity, operated only in the warmer months of July and August, but by 1913 the novelty had worn off and it closed down.

At the junction of Kentish Town Road and Prince

141. *The Palace, Kentish Town Road, in 1913.*

142. *The Gaisford, at the junction of Gaisford Street and Kentish Town Road.*

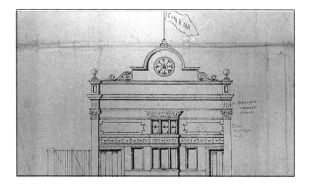

THE POPULAR

GARDEN CINEMA

PRINCE OF WALES ROAD, Opposite the Baths, KENTISH TOWN.

The only Open-air Animated Pictures in London.

MONDAY, JULY 31st, and during the week,

A SPECIAL SERIES OF PICTURES,

ILLUSTRATING—

Life in the King's Service

(AFLOAT AND ASHORE),

Selections from the following will be shown during the week:

Training of British Bluejackets
(at Whale Island, Portsmouth).

The Royal Naval Review at Spithead
(by GEORGE V., our Sailor King).

Trooping the Colours at Whitehall
(London's Greatest Military Pageant).

Scenes with Our Indian Army

The Pageant of "Our Empire"
(A Thrilling and Patriotic Picture).

A Grand Coronation Series
will be shown by Special Request.

MILITARY AIRSHIP MANŒUVRES

THE INVESTITURE OF H.R.H. THE PRINCE OF WALES
AT CARNARVON CASTLE.

Scenes with Our Territorial Forces
in Camp and Field.

Naval & Military Competitions.   Dancing the Hornpipe.
Gun Drill Displays, &c., &c.

The Programme will be interspersed with Humorous Pictures.

SPECIAL MUSIC.   SONGS.   ORIGINAL EFFECTS.

☞ Continuous Performance Nightly from 8 till 11.
GATES OPEN 7.30.

Admission 3d.   Children under 12, 2d.

A few Reserved Seats, 6d.

SPECIAL SUNDAY PROGRAMME AT 8 TILL 10.30.

Admission 3d.   Children under 12, 2d.

Printers—HUGGINS & Co., 250, High Street, Camden Town, N.W.

143. *Advertisement for the Garden Cinema in Prince of Wales Road, c.1911.*

144. The Forum, Highgate Road, soon after its opening in 1934.

of Wales Road stood The Palace, later the Gaumont. Its building, which had a narrow entrance, but extended across the backs of several shops, still survives. This opened in 1913 and closed in 1959. When the mayor of St Pancras officiated at the installation of a new sound system for talkies in 1930, he claimed that "The Palace is to be congratulated on possessing such an up-to-date apparatus and the management on their enterprising policy... the privilege of seeing and hearing such a picture would cost a guinea in New York, in the West End 5s 9d but here the price was as low as 6d!"

Further up the road at 303/305 was the Electric Alhambra, from 1911 to c.1918. This included a tea room with a separate entrance in Holmes Road accessible to ladies and children if they didn't wish to go through the cinema. Later the site was redeveloped by Marks & Spencer.

Gospel Oak had its own cinema – The Lismore at 37/39 Lismore Road. It seated 500 and had an orchestra, but its off-centre location limited its life to the years 1914-17. The forecourt of the block of flats

called Ludham now covers its site.

The best known of Kentish Town cinemas was the Forum in Highgate Road. Built in 1934 during the golden age of cinema building, it had a seating capacity of nearly 2,200. Its architect was John Stanley Beard, who over twenty years earlier had designed The Palace noted above. On the first floor there was a tea room and dance floor. In 1935 it became part of the ABC chain of theatres but not until 1963 was the old Forum name dropped. The cinema closed in 1970, for a time housed bingo and dancing, and during the 1980s it became a venue for the Town and Country Music Club. In 1992 it became the Forum again, under the management of the Mean Fiddler organisation and is now a highly successful rock and roll venue.

The last cinema to begin in Kentish Town and the last to close was The Venus, housed in the church hall of St Andrew's Greek Orthodox church at the corner of Kentish Town Road and Rochester Road. This opened in 1970 and was mainly used to present arthouse films; it closed in 1975.

145. *The Claudius Ash false teeth factory in Anglers Lane.*

Factories Hidden Away

CLAUDIUS ASH

There have not been many factories in Kentish Town, despite the proximity of the railway lands, but a number have been occupied by some very distinguished firms.

The most unusual company was that of Claudius Ash, which made false teeth in Anglers Lane. Ash was originally a silversmith in the West End, but began making false teeth in silver and gold at a time when the only alternative were those taken from corpses. By 1840 he was described as a manufacturer of 'mineral' teeth. A contemporary description of the process of making them noted that, "After calcination, the minerals were crushed into small pieces, ground dry and finally pestled in a mortar under water until they were absolutely gritless, like the finest white cream; this was then dried and stored in sealed jars until required." The material was then moulded to the appropriate shape.

The workshops in Anglers Lane were built in 1864. Here, with the aid of a steam engine and a kiln, the teeth were made and fired. In the 1880s the firm had branches as far afield as St Petersburg, Paris, Berlin, Vienna and New York; by 1915 it had a presence in 24 major cities including Cairo and Constantinople. In 1905 it was sufficiently profitable to go public with a share capital of £1 million.

The firm merged with a rival in 1924 and became the Amalgamated Dental Company. The Anglers Lane factory was vacated in 1965, although much of the old building survives.[1]

MAKING PIANOS

Camden and Kentish Town were famous for their piano factories. The most prominent in Kentish Town was that of John Brinsmead, whose factory was in Grafton Road. This vast building was said in 1904 to produce a piano every hour at prices ranging from 33 to 300 guineas. Brinsmead was born in Devon in 1814, the son of a farmer, and like a number of piano makers came into the trade via cabinet making. He began making pianos in Windmill Street, Tottenham Court Road in 1837, with just one apprentice as an employee. At the height of his activities in Kentish Town he had three hundred employees.

He and his wife – they married in 1837 – lived a long time. Both died at the age of 93 at their house in Albert Street, Camden Town.

146. John Brinsmead.

147. The main Brinsmead factory. The company had premises in Grafton Road, Ryland Road and Perren Street.

148. The Rowney artists' materials factory in Malden Crescent.

Piano making was a seasonal trade. Charles Booth in his *Life and Labour of the People of London* (1903) noted that the standard working week was 54-56 hours in winter and 48 in summer, but this was often reduced to 30. During busy periods men often worked to midnight. He also noted that factories had, of necessity, to be quite warm, which occasioned much drinking by the workers.

Chappell's had a piano factory at the junction of Belmont Street and Chalk Farm Road, and Allison Pianos occupied a good part of the west side of Charlton Kings Road from at least 1892.

Cabinet making in a big way was to be found in the Highgate Road, where Maple's built a large 'steam cabinet works' in 1899, displacing a row of houses between Greenwood Place and Carkers Lane. This building is now occupied by various furniture firms. Further up the road was Shand-Kydd's wallpaper factory – the Shand-Kydd family home, at least in this part of London, was Sidney House, which once occupied the site of the flats on the corner of Croftdown Road. The wallpaper factory now houses, more exotically, oriental carpet importers.

Coincidentally, as far as one can tell, the two largest manufacturers of artists' materials built their factories in Kentish Town. Rowney's factory, designed by Ebbetts and Cobb, was in Malden Crescent, and the Winsor & Newton building was in Spring Place.

149. Rescuing a dog and her pups after a Kentish Town bombing.

150. The ARP motor depot at Gospel Oak.

Time of War

By the time the first bombs fell on Kentish Town in 1940, there were in the borough of St Pancras 37 ARP posts, 8 First Aid Posts and 4 ARP Depots, 12,000 shelters in basements, and 3,000 in back gardens.[1]

On 8 September 1940 bombs fell on Bartholomew Road and Busby Place. During the blitz which followed the next year there were many casualties at Camelot House, Kentish Town, and damage was also done to the North-Western Polytechnic. During the night of one of the heaviest raids on London, 16 April 1941, a mine fell on Montague Tibbles House (Penshurst) in Prince of Wales Road and 16 people were killed.

By the end of hostilities there had been 1278 'air raid incidents' in St Pancras, 1,576 houses were demolished, 1,696 badly damaged, 1,744 uninhabitable, and another 13,825 had blast damage. As to casualties and deaths, 1,443 people had been seriously injured and 957 killed.

A number of areas were very badly hit. West Kentish Town, presumably for its proximity to vital railway interlinks, suffered the most, especially around Leybourne Road, Hawley Road and Clarence Way and in the Castlehaven Road area – Lord Stallard fought for many years during his time on Camden Council to have the bomb damaged area turned into a recreational space, an aspiration only partially realised. Other more specific bomb sites may be deduced from in-fill architecture. The top end of St Alban's Villas and the pub next door, in Highgate Road, were destroyed, as were parts of Woodsome Road and York Rise. Gospel Oak School was hit, which explains the new school building on Mansfield Road. The pre-fabricated flats opposite the reservoir in Dartmouth Park Hill are on the site of houses destroyed, and so are some developments in Spencer Rise and Churchill Road.

151. An ARP Wardens' Post.

152. Practising the use of gas masks at Kentish Town Day Nursery.

The St Pancras Rent Strike

In the late summer of 1960 media attention was often focused on a Council flat in Kennistoun House, Leighton Road, for it was here that Don Cook, a tenants' leader, lived behind a guard of pickets, barricades and barbed wire. Cook was both the leader of the famous St Pancras Rent Strike and a victim of the cause, for he was eventually evicted.

The story has its roots in the pre-War Act which introduced controlled rents for thousands of private tenancies. These rents, increasingly unrealistic, were still operative in the 1950s until the Conservative government passed several measures, including the Rent Act of 1956, to enable landlords to charge a market rent for their properties. But by then, with landlords disinclined to invest money in properties that did not make a sensible return, whole swathes of London housing had been blighted. This particularly affected West Kentish Town, where the standard of housing was poor to begin with. So much slum property made it even more likely that borough councils, particularly active ones like St Pancras, would buy up, knock down and build estates.

But with the freeing of rent controls in the mid 1950s the value of house property began to climb and the cost to St Pancras Council of acquiring land and houses consequently rose. The Council continued to demolish and build and the burden on the Housing Revenue Account, to which the costs of acquisition, building and interest charges were debited, grew alarmingly. They were beginning to outweigh by a considerable margin the revenue from rents which themselves were already subsidised. The intention of the Labour Council was pretty well known – it was to control much of the residential property in the borough – house ownership was regarded as anti-social, and private landlords were anathema. This genuinely-held enthusiasm for borough control stemmed, in part, from pre-War conditions when there was little alternative to privately rented occupation in very sub-standard houses: a large percentage of houses west of Kentish Town Road had no baths, but did have outside lavatories and shared kitchens. In the 1930s, during the well-organised heyday of the London County Council, it seemed to many that municipal control of the housing stock was essential, and when after the War borough councils were encouraged to build quickly a number took the matter very seriously indeed.

St Pancras Council in 1956 was led by a charismatic man called John Lawrence. He had a powerful and engaging presence, and despite his militancy he had the loyalty of most of his Labour colleagues on the Council and in the constituency Labour parties. At least in the beginning. For although it was easy enough for the Party to nail 'housing is a social service' to its banner, some members were in difficulty when it came to the finer print. Lawrence had no intention at all of "complying either with the spirit or letter of the new Tory housing laws",[1] and in 1956 set a maximum rent for Council tenants which in a good number of cases was less than the modest rents then being paid. This was the same year that the government abolished building subsidies to borough councils and in which the deficit on the Housing Revenue Account grew from £30,000 to £95,000. These do not now seem large amounts, but the value of money then may be assessed by the fact that the usual rent for a three-bedroomed flat in Kentish Town was £1.75p a week.

The councillors and their local parties decided to confront the government. The North St Pancras Labour Party at that time had a virtually windowless headquarters in Gordon House Road and in this airless and dreary hall the matter was discussed at very great length a number of times, but there was no serious opposition to the Lawrence-led policy.

In March 1958 the District Auditor surcharged Labour councillors for not raising rents. They appealed successfully, but in 1959 were surcharged again: by the financial year 1959/60 the deficit had risen to a remarkable £303,336.

The situation in St Pancras had been watched anxiously by the national Labour Party at Transport House, who were not only concerned about the rent policy adopted by the Council, but by the notorious flying of the Red Flag above St Pancras Town Hall on May Day. It was their view that the militancy which had caused such a national furore had to be controlled. There were many accusations that the local parties and the Council were now led by Communists, though there was not much evidence of that.

In 1958 the Labour Party expelled Lawrence and thirteen borough councillors. These included Jock Stallard, a life-long Labour Party member, who was later readmitted, became MP for North St Pancras and eventually was made Lord Stallard when his constituency was reshaped.

It was hardly surprising after this turmoil that in the following year the Conservatives, under Cllr Tony Prior, won control of St Pancras with the aim of reducing the deficit on the Housing Revenue Account. A maximum rent was set, and below that tenants were means tested as to their ability to pay. The 'means test' was, for many people, more obnoxious than the rent increases. Typically, on a three-bedroomed flat the maxiumum weekly rent went up from £1 15s 0d to £2 14s 3d.

EGGS FLUNG AT MAYOR

By BRIAN HITCHEN

COUNCILLORS were pelted with rotten eggs by tenants of council homes at a meeting in London last night.

There was uproar for twenty minutes at St. Pancras Borough Council's monthly meeting while the public gallery was cleared and after the demonstration a resolution was passed **BANNING** the public from the next three meetings at the Town Hall.

Two "commandos" from the local council tenants' association led by Mr. Don Cook, 38, went along to the meeting to hear a report on the working of a scheme in which the tenants pay rent according to their wages. Some rents have been doubled.

Rumpus over rents plan

small crowbars to force the chains.

~~One demonstrator Ken~~

the rent scheme against which they are protesting and I will see it through

153. How the Daily Mirror saw events in 1960.

A United Tenants Association was formed which included on its committee Don Cook, an AEU shop steward. This organised a number of marches to the Town Hall to protest at the rent scheme. In November the UTA adopted a policy of withholding rents and in January 1960 the Council began to issue eviction notices to 1100 tenants who were still not paying rent. In February the *St Pancras Chronicle* reported that only 68 were still holding out, but by June only three tenants were left and, without a legal case, liable to be evicted.

There then began the remarkable events in Leighton Road.[2] All day and night people were gathered around Kennistoun House, some as active supporters, some just out of curiosity. The Fire Brigades Union declined to assist in any eviction and the uneasy situation in Leighton Road continued for several weeks. It came to an end at 6.45am on 22 September when bailiffs and police secured the eviction of Don Cook and his family.

Don Cook would today be startled, and almost certainly outraged, to see the clutch of estate agents' boards outside his block of flats at the moment.

Famous Names

Once Kentish Town had lost its rural attractions there was scarcely time for it to become respectably urban, let alone fashionable, before the onslaught of cheap housing and railways made it an unlikely choice for famous names. As we have seen, an establishment figure like William Stukeley chose the village to retire to in the 1760s; in 1813 Joseph Shepherd Munden (1758-1832), a well known actor, occupied Croft Lodge in Highgate Road, now part of the property of La Sainte Union Convent, before moving to the smaller house next door to the north. Henry Bessemer (1813-98), immensely rich and to be even richer from his invention of a process to mass-produce steel, moved into another house on the site of the Convent in 1851, which he renamed Charlton House, after his birthplace in Hertfordshire.

Off Highgate Road just north of the railway bridge are the two small streets Wesleyan Place and Mortimer Terrace, built by the Mortimer family – before the railway was built these connected up with Carrol Place to the south to form a rectangle. At No 13 Mortimer Terrace in 1820, Leigh Hunt (1784-1859) was the ratepayer. During that year John Keats (1795-1821), then alarmingly ill, came to lodge in Wesleyan Place, but his condition was such that he moved into Hunt's overcrowded house where he could be cared

155. Joseph Shepherd Munden.

154. John Keats.

156. Leigh Hunt.

for. Until recently Mortimer Terrace faced a railway embankment, but in those days it looked out onto the fields of Mortimer's farm across to Hampstead. The much lesser-known poet, Coventry Patmore (1823-96), lived in The Grove in the 1850s. Douglas Jerrold (1803-57), writer and dramatist, spent two of his few affluent years – 1839-40 – at Craven Place North, a terrace of houses north of St John's Church in Highgate Road.

Undoubtedly the most famous name to live in Kentish Town is Karl Marx. The penurious Marx family had been staying in small, furnished rooms in Dean Street, Soho while he researched at the British Museum. In 1856 his wife inherited £150 from an uncle and soon afterwards another inheritance enabled the family to move up to Grafton Terrace, near Maitland Park Road. They settled at what became no. 46 – the house is still there, but without a plaque. Here, as Jenny Marx recalled, they "slept in our own beds for the first time, sat on our own chairs and even had a parlour with second-hand furniture". They paid £36 a year in rent, but even so they were financially stretched. He wrote to his friend Engels the following year that "Today I am actually worse off than I was five years ago when I was wallowing in the very quintessence of filth".

The 1860 parish map shows that side of Grafton Terrace facing an open field. Evidently, the road was still not made up and in winter was a muddy path. Marx confided to Engels that it was difficult for him to work because he was always trying to make some money, and there were domestic problems: "My wife's nerves are quite ruined by the filth." The year 1864 was an important one for Marx. His finances were saved by the deaths of his mother and an old friend, who both left him money. The family moved round the corner to 1 Modena Villas, subsequently renumbered 1 Maitland Park Road, a house built on the estate of the Orphan Working School. Also in that year he emerged as a leader of the International Working Men's Association at a time when there was considerable popular unrest in the country. Marx wrote the draft rules for this organisation in his house at Maitland Park.[1]. It was also while at this house that 'Charles' Marx was nominated as one of the Vestry's unpaid constables. The first volume of his major work, *Das Kapital*, appeared in 1873. In 1875 his name appears appealing against his rate assessment when he had moved to 41 Maitland Park Road. It was in this house that Marx died in 1883. Both of his houses in this road have now gone, replaced by a London County Council estate after the last war.

The author of *Three Men in a Boat*, Jerome K. Jerome (1859-1927), lived at an unknown date at 15 Oakfield Crescent, quite near to Marx's house in Grafton Terrace. Another writer of a classic book was born at 21 Malden Crescent, the daughter of a local doctor

157. *Karl Marx.*

158. *15 Oakfield Crescent, off Wellesley Road, the castellated home of Jerome K. Jerome. The street no longer exists.*

who, she later related, was often the worse for drink. The daughter was Stella Gibbons (1902-89), author of *Cold Comfort Farm*, who was to spend much of her life (from 1937 onwards) at 19 Oakeshott Avenue, on the Holly Lodge Estate.

The peripatetic writer, George Orwell, spent six months from August 1935 in Kentish Town at 50 Lawford Road, where he shared a 3-roomed flat with his friend Rayner Heppenstall. The tram driver and his wife downstairs complained that Orwell kept them awake at night with his typing. In 1936 he left to take on a Gollancz commission to write about the depressed north of England – his best creative years were before him.[2]

John Betjeman (1906-84), was born in Lissenden Mansions, and when he was one year old the family moved up to 31 Highgate West Hill. Betjeman's poem *Parliament Hill Fields* is an account of a tram ride he took when he was seven or eight. He begins it opposite Kentish Town Station, where the railway rumbles underneath the main road into the then smokey hinterland of railway sheds, cattle handling stations, coal depots, repair shops and junctions. He writes of the premises of Charrington, Sells, Dale and Co., "Nuts and nuggets in the window, trucks along the line below". He is referring to a coal dealer's shop opposite the station which had a window containing a large-scale model train filled with coal. This will be remembered by many people, as it was still there

159. *Stella Gibbons.*

160. *Parliament Hill Mansions in Lissenden Gardens. John Betjeman was born in Lissenden Mansions in the same road.*

161. *Zwaniger's, the German bakers at 385 Kentish Town Road, at the beginning of this century.*

in the 1960s. Behind the shop were coal depots supplying the firm, and also cattle depots, where cattle were off-loaded to herd along Leighton Road and Brecknock Road, down to the Metropolitan Cattle Market off York Way. It is odd to think of these processions of animals along Leighton Road which went on until the 1930s.

Betjeman continues:

"Rocked past Zwaniger the baker's, and the terrace blackish brown,
And the curious Anglo-Norman parish church of Kentish Town.

Zwaniger's was one of the many German bakers in London before the First World War. They and others were subject to popular persecution during the war and many went out of business – the Zwanigers changed their name to Cordingley.[3]

The 'terrace blackish brown' is an early Kentish Town terrace, probably of the 1790s, called Craven Place South, built by Thomas Greenwood, whose name is commemorated by a small turning near the Forum. The terrace, when built, extended across the site of the old cinema. The 'Anglo-Norman' church is, of course, St John's.

Other famous residents have included the Pre-Raphaelite artist, Ford Madox Brown (1821-93) at what is now 56 Fortess Road; nearby Dr Southwood Smith (1790-1861), one of the founders of sanitary science, lived at no. 40. Richard D'Oyly Carte (1844-1901), the producer of the famous Gilbert & Sullivan operas, is noted in the street directory of 1884 at 2 Dartmouth Park Road, after he had moved from smaller premises on the site of the parade of shops at the foot of Highgate West Hill facing Swains Lane. Charles Grignion, a celebrated engraver (1717-1810), died in Grove Terrace and was buried at St John's church. George Grossmith (1874-1935), the actor-manager, is shown at 15 Maitland Park Villas in 1874, and Thomas Idris, founder of the soft drinks company which had its works in Royal College Street, lived at 4 St Alban's Villas. The scientist, Oliver Lodge (1851-1940), moved from Holloway to 11 Burghley Road in the early 1880s. Another Burghley Road resident was Kwame Nkrumah, the first Prime Minister of Ghana, who lived at no. 60 from 1945-47. The artist and inventor, Cornelius Varley (1781-1873) is shown in an 1867 directory at 337 Kentish Town Road in premises with Samuel Varley, a telegraph engineer.

Ideals and Actualities

In 1977, when Gillian Tindall wrote her perceptive history of Kentish Town, *The Fields Beneath*, she excoriated planners and councillors for their wilful destruction of much of Kentish Town since the war. It was a damning piece of criticism. By then much of the damage was done and little development remained in the pipeline. Is there, twenty years later and looking back, any reason to dispute the case she made?

Has the extensive municipalisation of Kentish Town served it badly? It might help to compare Kentish Town with Camden Town, where demolition and development has been much more limited. Both places were built up at about the same time, both severely blighted by railways, both for nearly a hundred years were havens of cheap rents, the houses multi-occupied by families drawn to work in the great wen of London. Yet Camden Town was and remains the more vibrant place, both culturally and economically. Kentish Town has had no theatre, it has no cinemas, and even in the current boom in eating out, has few restaurants. Chain stores and supermarkets have largely deserted the high street and there is not even a proliferation of estate agents.

In comparison with Camden Town, Kentish Town is a commercial backwater. Many residents probably prefer it that way and despite the congestion of parked cars and traffic there are many benefits to living in the well-formed streets to the east of Kentish Town Road.

But in West Kentish Town we have seen complete transformation, and it was this that Gillian Tindall was talking about. She pointed out that after the first post-war years slum-clearance was not the driving force in this extraordinary sequence of demolition and rebuilding. It was succeeded by 'comprehensive development', which became a symbol of political rectitude, especially among Labour Party councillors. For a time no street was safe, let alone those which had outside lavatories and no baths.

Housing in West Kentish Town was indeed very run down and inadequate. Sometimes families shared a single tap. Sometimes communal cooking facilities were on landings. Damp walls, damp floorboards were commonplace. The architecture was generally undistinguished and the houses not worth saving on that account. The Council had some choices. It could demolish and rebuild with streets, demolish and rebuild in estates, or renovate and convert. The third choice was never a possibility, and so far as I know was never even toyed with – there was no political

will to do so and there was no professional competence to carry it out. Only one choice, the second, was promoted for it suited and satisfied a conjunction in power and influence of two groups of people.

One group was the leadership of the local Labour parties. For most of the twenty years after the last war this consisted of men and women who grew up between the wars – their political reactions were formed during that period. Many had experienced the sort of housing which prevailed in West Kentish Town. Here, the houses were built sub-standard, and their decline was fostered by private landlords reluctant to repair them, and even more reluctant once rent control made them uneconomic. Areas such as this, in contrast to the well-maintained estates that the London County Council had pioneered between the wars, served to confirm not just a belief in municipal housing, but the desirability of estates. It seemed then to any Labour Party activist that council estates held the key to future working-class living, for in those days working-class ownership of property was neither contemplated or possible. A number of schemes were built in the 1950s and the early 1960s, mostly red-brick faced by monotonous balconies (Clarence Way for example), but the bulk of development in West Kentish Town was still to come.

In the later 1960s another group of people appeared when Camden (and other London boroughs) began to employ a new breed of professional advisor – planners. Their like had not been encountered before at borough council level where planning, if any, was done by the Borough Architect in consultation with the Borough Engineer. But Sir Patrick Abercrombie's Greater London Plan, drawn up even while the war still raged, created a climate in which 'planning' was both desirable and necessary when the bombed and slum areas were eventually cleared. Neighbourhoods were to be 'zoned' so that industry and residents did not live side by side and new major roads through London were proposed – plans for these were still blighting Camden Town in the 1970s.

Planners had the enthusiasm of youth. Their icon was Le Corbusier, their tutors wedded to garden city ideals, and their mission was to transform London. They found willing partners in the councillors who then held sway, and they arrived in force in 1965 when boroughs were reorganised as larger units and Camden was formed. Planners had no interest in the conversion of sub-standard accommodation – there were then no brownie points to be gathered in the profession's journals for such work. That it could be done, given the will, is shown today by Hadley and Healey Streets, Quadrant Grove and Oak Village, where similar houses survive and flourish.

The attraction of West Kentish Town was that the property was cheap to buy up. Because it was already sub-standard and blighted by well-broadcast Council intentions, it became worse, so that the borough found little difficulty in obtaining comprehensive purchase orders. The sluminess was evident for all to see and therefore the political fulfilment was even more fulfilling. Expert planning consultants were invited to propose the eventual form of the area. The old street pattern was largely abolished in favour of a layout of blocks. 'Pedestrian walkways' replaced streets in this new form of living, where through traffic was inhibited and residents, as though on a village green, chatted to their neighbours on these elevated paths. Their proposals were not insensitive and recognised that common open spaces did not really compensate for loss of private gardens. But by then the die was cast, for blocks rather than streets were the preferred solution. Furthermore, all this conformed to government encouragement – councils were urged to build high and in blocks if they could.

The consequence has been that the estates, architecturally, are inward looking. And, as Gillian Tindall pointed out, by discouraging through traffic they inevitably discourage outsiders from entering on foot.

There is nothing new in observing that the development of such estates since the last war has created and emphasised a social difference between 'renting tenants' and 'private owners'. As Ms Tindall commented, "the supreme irony of council estate construction is that it has ultimately proved socially divisive and anti-egalitarian". If anything, since she wrote those words, the pressures to own property, rather than to rent it (especially from the Council), have increased. The 'right-to-buy' legislation has even more isolated the tower blocks where ownership of a flat is less desirable if only because of the practical difficulties of maintenance.

The tradition of renting, once firmly established within the working-class, has in this way come under attack. Though it is common in all classes in Europe and America, it has somehow become an admission of social instability in London. This bias will pass – housing associations are helping to make renting respectable again.

This author, as a former borough councillor, was part and parcel for a time of the enthusiasm to municipalise West Kentish Town. In the process it was possible to acquire socialist credentials, and it was only in the very late 1960s that doubts emerged, at least for some councillors, as to the wisdom of it all. The Planning Department wanted to knock down virtually everything in the area, including, for example the two delightful villas in Malden Crescent that still face Prince of Wales Road. These were saved because councillors dug their heels in against the officers. Things came to a head in the matter of Oak Village in Gospel Oak, which the officers and many Labour councillors wanted to demolish. The plan-

ners felt that this would be a logical fusion of their schemes around Lismore Circus and a good many Labour councillors were hostile to the private owners who had surprisingly modernised the tiny Oak Village houses. The Village was saved by a whisker, by cross-voting of councillors on the Planning and Development Committee. But by then the belief in 'estates' was waning and a positive dislike of high blocks (reinforced by the dreadful catastrophe of the gas explosion at Ronan Point in the East End) was growing. From that time on planners had a diminished reputation.

The 'right-to-buy' legislation of the 1980s effectively put an end to Council building developments, but in truth they were virtually finished. It had become too expensive and public opinion, now articulate, would not stand for many more. Ironically, Camden gave up building just as British Rail were at last releasing more surplus land in Kentish Town. Here, imaginative planning and landscaping could have produced a creditable scheme which for the first time since the fields were last visible might have connected the disparate halves of Kentish Town.

It is depressing now to walk to the end of Carkers Lane, off Highgate Road, and see that this opportunity is being squandered. A mish-mash of light industrial and commercial development is taking place. Mean buildings and tawdry car parks meet the eye. The vista up to Parliament Hill is wasted. Camden has, it seems, no role in this and just as railways had *carte blanche* to invade the neighbourhood in the nineteenth century, so it seems they have leeway to develop their land for whatever profit might be going regardless of any larger interests.

In the nineteenth century all sorts of missions established themselves in West Kentish Town to ameliorate poverty, illiteracy and intemperance. In the later twentieth century their amended role has been undertaken by neighbourhood centres and advice centres. The Interchange Studio, which began as Inter Action, promotes local activities, particularly amongst children and we have them, and Camden Council, to thank for the unexpected pleasures of the Kentish Town City Farm off Grafton Road. When Gillian Tindall wrote her book, the preoccupation of the worried middle-classes was that working-class children had stopped playing spontaneous or organised games, not only because the streets were no longer safe to use, but because the lure of television had taken away their appetite for such things. Twenty years on the concern is that the lonely pleasures of video games, and impersonal communication through the Internet, prevent children inter-reacting with their peers. On the face of it the need for Interchange and similar neighbourhood groups has not diminished. The worry is that the concept of 'community' they believe in is being left behind.

Sources

THE EARLY VILLAGE
[1] See Charles Lee: *St Pancras Church and Parish*, 14-16 (1955).
[2] This parish church has been made redundant by the Church of England and, at the time of writing, is occupied by the Christ Apostolic Church UK. For the purposes of this book the old church dedication of St John the Baptist will be used.
[3] *St Pancras Vestry Minutes*, 20 August 1794.

MANORS AND VESTRY
[1] But see p.26, where Mr Woodhouse's witchhunt story of 1703 states that a workhouse already existed in the area.
[2] See p. 21 for more about this house.

ELUSIVE HOUSES
[1] See, for example, an investigation by Gillian Tindall in *Camden History Review* No. 4 (c.1976).
[2] 'The Woodhouse Journal', a book of notes and miscellaneous comments about St Pancras parish compiled in the first decade of the eighteenth century by William Woodhouse JP. This volume is now in the Local Studies and Archive Centre of the London Borough of Camden.
[3] Reprinted in *Survey of London*, Vol XIX 'Old St Pancras and Kentish Town', 27 (1938).
[4] The Survey of 1649 details the fields in the demesne, including that occupied by the manor house. By comparing the acreage of those fields and, where indicated on the Survey, their location, against the field layout on the earliest reliable map, it is possible to arrive at this conclusion. The map in question is that made by John Thompson from about 1796, and published about 1800.
[5] The conjunction of river, workhouse and a view north to Kentish Town Chapel does not seem to be possible, judging from the 1800 map.
[6] Heal Collection A6/28.
[7] Heal Collection A6/29, copied from British Museum Addl MS 5176, dated and signed 10 June 1727.
[8] The possibility that these remains depicted by King may be the vestiges of Bruges' house was first suggested by Gillian Tindall in *Camden History Review* No. 4.

THE RIVER FLEET
[1] F.W.M. Draper: 'The Place Names of Ken Wood and Kentish Town' in *London Topographical Record*, Vol. XXII, 27-8 (1965).
[2] Tottenhall Manor Records 1321, as transcribed by Pauline Sidell for the Camden History Society. Guildhall Library MS 25,346/4.

A GENTLEMAN'S RETREAT
[1] Robert Milligan is shown as occupier of Kentish Town House on Thompson's c.1800 map of St Pancras parish.
[2] Paul Callan: *A 'Wanstead House' in Highgate* (1997).
[3] Gillian Tindall: *The Fields Beneath*, 122-123 (1977)
[4] Heal Collection A5/69, newspaper cutting 1764.
[5] John Richardson: *Highgate, Its history since the Fifteenth Century*, 22 (1983)

THE MAKING OF THE JUNCTION ROAD
[1] I am indebted to Simon Morris for information in this chapter.

GOOD INTENTIONS
[1] According to Mr Heal the plan was in the Chantry Rolls of the Augmentation Office, an old copy of which is in the Musgrave MSS in the British Library. Mr Heal's beautiful copy of this is in the Heal Collection A6/29.
[2] See article by Eric Corner on the Orphan Working School in *Camden History Review* 21 (1997).
[3] Charles E. Lee: 'The St Pancras Church Lands Trust', transcript of a talk given by Mr Lee on 9 November 1973.

SCHOOLDAYS
[1] Information from Mrs Ann Currie.
[2] See article by Gillian Tindall, 'School Skeleton' in *Camden History Society Newsletter* 60 (July 1980).

INN PLACES
[1] Frederick Miller: *St Pancras Past and Present* (1874)
[2] *Ibid*, 286.

MR KING AND HIS PANORAMA
[1] *Survey of London*, Vol. XIX, 'Old St Pancras and Kentish Town', 33 (1938)
[2] *The Kentish Town Panorama* drawn by James Frederick King, with commentary by John Richardson, published by the London Topographical Society (1986). Obtainable from the Society, or else from the Local History and Archives Centre, Holborn Library, Theobalds Road, WC1.

DIVIDED BY LINES
[1] A house called The Retreat is shown at 95 Highgate Road in contemporary street directories.
[2] Article by David Thomas in *Camden History Society Newsletter* 95 (May 1986).

A BURST OF CHURCHES
[1] Frederick Miller: *St Pancras Past and Present*, 218-226 (1874).
[2] Much of the information about Methodists in Kentish Town comes from 'The Spiritual Strength of Kentish Town' by John S. Ellis in *Camden History Review* 6 (1978).
[3] Gillian Tindall: *The Fields Beneath*, 156 (1977).
[4] Information re Highgate Baptist Church comes from its centenary booklet, by Ann Winser, published in 1977.
[5] See article by Jane Cox, 'Spreading the gospel in Gospel Oak: All Hallows, the Cathedral of North London', in *Camden History Review* 20 (1996).

BODY AND MIND
[1] Information for this section on libraries is taken from 'Prayers at Highgate' by James G. Ollé in *Library World*, Autumn 1968.
[2] See *87 Holmes Road* by Cicely Herbert and Ann Langton (c.1990).

TRADING PLACES
[1] Article by Gillian Tindall in *Camden History Society Newsletter* 45 (Jan 1978).
[2] *Ibid*.
[3] *JS100: The Story of Sainsbury's*, published by Sainsbury's (1969).
[4] Desmond Whyman, 'Butchers' shops in Kentish Town' in *Camden History Review* 20 (1996).
[5] Vivian Carter: *The Romance of Rotary in London*, 118 (1947).
[6] Retold by Gillian Tindall in *Camden History Society Newsletter* 53 (May 1979).

THE SOCIAL SIDE
[1] Information for this chapter has been taken with permission from *The Cinemas of Camden*, by Mark Aston, published by the Local Studies and Archives Centre of the London Borough of Camden (1997).

FACTORIES HIDDEN AWAY
[1] Information from article by David Thomas in *Camden History Society Newsletter* 94 (Mar. 1986).

TIME OF WAR
[1] See 'Air raid precautions in St Pancras 1935-1945' by Robin Woolven, in *Camden History Review* 16 (1989).

THE ST PANCRAS RENT STRIKE
[1] See David Mathieson: *The St Pancras Rent Strike 1960, a study in consensus politics* (1986), published by the Labour Party. This summarises the sequence of events.
[2] Similar scenes were enacted at Silverdale, a block of flats on Hampstead Road, where another tenants' leader, Arthur Rowe, was also holding out. He was evicted on the same morning as Cook.

FAMOUS NAMES
[1] Asa Briggs: *Marx in London*, 69 (1982).
[2] John Thompson: *Orwell's London*, 45 (1984).
[3] Information ex Gillian Tindall.

Further Reading

Ashton, J: *The Fleet* (1888).

Aston, Mark: *The Cinemas of Camden* (1997).

Barnes, E.G: *The Rise of the Midland Railway* (1966)

Barker, T.C. and Robbins, M: *A History of London Transport* (1963).

Barton, Nicholas: *The Lost Rivers of London* (rev. edn 1992)

Bennett, J: *Some Account of Kentish Town* (1821).

Briggs, Asa: *Marx in London* (1982).

Brown, Walter E: *The St Pancras Poor: a brief record of their treatment etc from 1718 to 1904* (1905).

Burchell, Doris: *Miss Buss's Other School* (1971).

Callan, Paul: *A 'Wanstead House' in Highgate* (1997).

Denyer, C.H. (ed):   *St Pancras Through the Ages* (1935).

Grosch, Alfred: *St Pancras Pavements* (1947).

Harrison, Walter: *A History of London* (1775).

Jenkins, Simon: *Landlords to London; the story of a capital and its growth* (1975).

Lee, Charles E: *St Pancras Church and Parish* (1955).

Lee, Charles E: *Sixty Years of the Northern Line* (1967).

London, Hugh Stanford: *The Life of William Bruges* (1960).

Lovell, Percy and Marcham, W. McB: *Survey of London,* 'Old St Pancras and
    Kentish Town' Vol. XIX (1938).

Marshall, Lesley: *Kentish Town: Its Past and Present* (1993).

Mathieson, David: *St Pancras Rent Strike: a study in consensus politics* (1986).

Mayhew, Henry: *London Labour and the London Poor* (1861).

Miller, Frederick: *St Pancras Past and Present*   (1874).

Norden, John: *Speculum Britanniae* (1549).

Olsen, Donald J: *Town Planning in London* (1964).

Palmer, Samuel: *St Pancras* (1870).

Piggot, Stuart: *William Stukeley* (1950).

Robbins, Michael: *A History of the North London Railway* (1946).

Scrimgeour, R.M. (ed.):   *The North London Collegiate School 1850-1950* (1950).

Thompson, John: *Orwell's London* (1984).

Tindall, Gillian: *The Fields Beneath: the history of one London village* (1977).

Winser, Ann: *Highgate Road Baptist Church centenary booklet*

Wiswould, Samuel: *The Charities of St Pancras* (1863).

MISCELLANEOUS SOURCES

King, James Frederick: *Kentish Town Panorama* (published in facsimile by London Topographical
    Society, with commentary by John Richardson, 1986).

St Pancras Parish Registers

St Pancras Vestry Minutes 1718-1889.

Cantelowes Court Rolls

The Woodhouse Journal (Local History Studies and Archives Centre).

Camden History Society Newsletter 1970 -

Camden History Review 1973 -

St Pancras Journal (published by Libraries Department) 1947 on, becoming *Camden Journal* in 1966.

Heal Collection at the Local Studies and Archives Centre

Index

Asterisks denote illustrations